THE ARGUMENT-
FREE MARRIAGE

THE ARGUMENT-FREE MARRIAGE

28 DAYS TO CREATING THE MARRIAGE YOU'VE ALWAYS WANTED WITH THE SPOUSE YOU ALREADY HAVE

FAWN WEAVER

NELSON
BOOKS

An Imprint of Thomas Nelson

Published in Nashville, Tennessee, by Nelson Books, an imprint of Thomas Nelson. Nelson Books and Thomas Nelson are registered trademarks of HarperCollins Christian Publishing, Inc.

Published in association with William K. Jensen Literary Agency.

Thomas Nelson titles may be purchased in bulk for educational, business, fund-raising, or sales promotional use. For information, please e-mail SpecialMarkets@ ThomasNelson.com.

This book is not intended to provide therapy, counseling, clinical advice or treatment, or to take the place of clinical advice or treatment from your professional counselor or mental health provider. Readers are advised to consult their own qualified health care provider regarding mental health, therapy, or counseling. Neither the publisher nor the author takes any responsibility for any possible consequences from any treatment, action, or application of information in this book to the reader.

Financial advice provided in this book is not intended to take the place of professional financial counseling. Neither the publisher nor the author takes responsiblity for any possible consequences of someone following said financial advice.

In some instances, names, dates, locations, and other identifying details have been changed to protect the identities and privacy of those mentioned in this book. Permission has been granted by all persons for the use of their personal stories and the adaptations that have been made.

Library of Congress Cataloging-in-Publication Data

Weaver, Fawn, 1976-

The argument-free marriage : 28 days to creating the marriage you've always wanted with the spouse you already have / Fawn Weaver.

pages cm

Includes bibliographical references.

ISBN 978-1-4002-0506-6

1. Marriage--Religious aspects--Christianity. 2. Conflict management--Religious aspects--Christianity. I. Title.

BV835.W3845 2015

248.8'44--dc23

2014047902

Printed in the United States of America

15 16 17 18 19 RRD 6 5 4 3 2 1

For Keith
Thank you for your friendship. Thank you for your love.
Thank you for helping me become the best version of me.
Thank you for always striving to be the best version of you.

CONTENTS

CONTENTS

FOREWORD

MOST OF US GOT MARRIED WHEN WE WERE "IN LOVE." WE were carried along by euphoric feelings that we anticipated would last forever. We fully intended to make each other happy for the rest of our lives. But for many of us, life did not go as planned. The euphoric feelings evaporated and were replaced by feelings of hurt, anger, and resentment. Marriage became one long series of arguments with a warm oasis here and there. Unfortunately, many couples never find their way back to emotional intimacy. Some choose divorce, others resign themselves to staying under the same roof, but living separate lives. Essentially they are roommates, though they are likely sleeping in separate rooms.

God did not ordain marriage to make people miserable. God ordained marriage because He knows that "two are better than one." Marriage is designed to be a mutually loving, caring, supportive relationship in which both husband and wife encourage each other to reach their potential for good in the world. When this happens, life is beautiful. This is the kind of marriage most of us desired when we said yes to marriage.

However, there is one major factor that keeps many of us from reaching this dream. In a word, it is *selfishness*. We are all ego-centric. There is a positive aspect of this—we feed ourselves, get proper rest, exercise, and seek to keep our bodies healthy. But, when self-centeredness becomes selfishness, then, we view all of life with the question: "What's in it for me?" This attitude becomes a major hurdle when it is carried into marriage.

Selfishness is the opposite of love. Love is giving for the bene-fit of another. Selfishness is demanding that others meet my needs. Two demanding people—two selfish people—will never have the marriage of which they dreamed. The attitude of love is the foundation upon which a healthy marriage is built. When both husband and wife are seeking the well-being of the other, they will build the marriage they have always wanted.

This kind of love is very different from the euphoria of the "in-love" experience. You did not work to "fall in love." It simply happened. But once the euphoria subsides (the average lifespan is two years), then you must decide to keep love alive. This kind of love begins with an attitude, a way of thinking. Love says, "I choose to seek your well-being. How may I help you?" Every day, you choose to live with an attitude of love or an attitude of selfishness.

This does not mean that I give no thought to my own well-being. Marriage is always a two-way street. We give and we receive. However, too many of us are waiting for our spouses to love us before we are willing to love them. We have failed to reckon with the reality that love stimulates love. It does not matter who starts the process. But when I choose to love you, I make it easier for you to love me.

Selfishness leads to arguments in which each of us is demand-ing that the other agree with us and do what we desire. Love is

seeking to understand the other's thoughts and feelings, to nego-
tiate differences, to focus on solutions rather than on winning
arguments. We respect each other as individuals worthy of our
time and energy. Two loving people will create a healthy marriage.

Having read the book you hold in your hands, I am convinced
that Fawn and Keith Weaver have chosen to walk the road of
love. That is why Fawn can write about "The Argument-Free
Marriage." You may be thinking what I thought when I first saw
the title: *Really?* I have been counseling couples for over thirty-five
years and not many couples have come into my office with an
argument-free marriage. In fact, most of them are there because
they are tired of arguing and don't know how to stop.

If you are willing to call a "cease-fire" on arguments for
twenty-eight days, and choose instead an attitude of love toward
each other, I believe that this book will help you move toward the
marriage you've always wanted. Don't expect perfection, but you
can expect growth. Fawn does not paint a primrose path. She is
realistic in her expectations and in her advice.

If your spouse is reluctant to join you, don't try to force him
or her. Rather, simply request that your spouse walk with you
for the first seven days and then decide if he or she wishes to
continue. Love makes requests, not demands.

Gary Chapman, Ph.D.
Author of *The Five Love Languages*

CAN YOU REALLY CREATE AN ARGUMENT-FREE MARRIAGE?

HAVE YOU EVER WONDERED WHAT YOUR MARRIAGE WOULD be like if you and your spouse didn't argue as much? Maybe you don't call it "arguing"—perhaps you call it "loud discussions" or "spats" or "airing out your differences" or, as I recently heard termed at a marriage conference, "intense fellowship." Whatever you call them, you know these disputes can eat away at your marriage, one harsh word at a time.

But what if your marriage could be *argument-free*? What if you could experience more peace, better communication, and more intimacy in your marriage?

An argument-free marriage is something few people talk about, and for good reason. Many don't think such a union exists. Maybe you, too, have your doubts. Is having an argument-free marriage even possible?

The answer is *yes*!

How can I be so sure that you and your spouse can create an argument-free marriage? Because when I married my husband, I was one of the most strong-willed, naturally argumentative

1

women you ever wanted to meet, and my husband, Keith, was and is one of the strongest and most determined men I've ever known. So if we can do it, I'm certain you can too.

LIVING PROOF OF AN ARGUMENT-FREE MARRIAGE

Anyone who knows Keith and me will tell you we have fun! We love life. We absolutely adore each other and can't seem to keep our hands to ourselves (in a good way). We've been married for more than a decade, but we're still as passionate as two newlyweds on their honeymoon and have never lost our attraction toward each other. We are always affectionate and remain vulnerable to each other.

Yet Keith and I have extremely different personalities. He is the diplomat of our family, works in government affairs, and carefully crafts every statement that leaves his mouth. In contrast, I am free-spirited, usually say what's on my mind, and am transparent about our lives. He likes to keep everything private. I don't mind sharing my heart with the whole world. I would rather sit down to write this book, while he'd rather read books about history, politics, and government. I can generally take a problem and come up with a solution within minutes. Keith will take the same problem, look at it from every angle, and then give several scenarios that could serve as possible solutions. I go from A to Z pretty quickly. His analytic nature causes him to pause between A and B, C and D, E and F (well, you get the picture).

Recently, as we were each considering the purchase of a Mini Countryman, I looked on the website and determined I wanted my Countryman to have two things: a white exterior and a center armrest (oddly enough, that wasn't standard). Keith, on the other hand, ruminated about it every day. And I mean every single day. He went to their website on no fewer than fifty occasions to create a new car on their app that allows potential purchasers to choose all the features. The first ten times I was genuinely interested in seeing the car he'd constructed online. After the twentieth time, I was definitely over it. I bought my Mini the same day I found one for a good price at a local dealer (in white with a center armrest). A couple of hours later, I sold the ten-year-old car I'd happily been driving for years.

How can two people who are so different in their approach to life and making decisions live so cohesively?

I know it's hard to believe, but Keith and I laugh, joke, play, travel, spend as many hours together as possible, and never, since marrying in 2003, have we fallen into an argument. In part, that's because we are so compatible, despite our differing personalities. But more than that, we have put in place some extremely helpful techniques and practical strategies that help us regularly communicate our differences without erupting in a fight.

Keith and I don't sweep issues under the rug and avoid arguments at all costs. As a matter of fact, in the beginning of our relationship, not arguing went completely against my natural instincts. Keith wins reasoned arguments and debates for a living. Either one of us could have done very well as a trial attorney. Yet by applying specific boundaries and principles to our marriage, we've managed to peaceably disagree on many things over the years while remaining iron-willed and strong-minded people with firm convictions about what we believe.

For the next twenty-eight days, I'll show you the tips and techniques Keith and I have implemented to experience the happiness, peace, intimacy, and transparency of an argument-free marriage. This book is an invitation into our marriage, to see how we've applied these principles in our own personal lives. As Keith read through the first draft of this book, he said, "You and I are mentioned so much throughout the book. That seems odd." Indeed it is, because we tend to like to deflect attention. But my response to him came quickly and with a smile, "The book is about an argument-free marriage. There's certainly not much other data available for this concept." Touché.

HOW CAN SPOUSES COEXIST WITHOUT ARGUING?

If you picked up this book thinking, *There is no way two people with different personalities, raised in different households, and with different upbringings can coexist without arguing,* please consider setting aside that idea, at least for the time it will take you to read these pages.

Keith and I not only have very different personalities; we couldn't have had more different upbringings. His parents divorced; my parents were Christian marriage counselors. His parents rarely, if ever, took him to church; my parents took my sisters and me every Sunday for the entire day. Keith turned out to be the most levelheaded person I know. I have always been a bit of a firecracker.

Some people enjoy fighting and engaging in endless debates that lead to arguments. I understand. I was that person. But marriage without arguments, fussing, and fighting can be so much better. Keith and I don't waste time being upset or yelling at each other or not speaking for days on end. Instead, we are able to spend our brief time on earth wrapping our arms around each other, going on romantic dates, joking and playing around, making love, sharing what's on our minds, building the life we most desire—together.

Several years ago, Keith and I created a wedding gift for one of my sisters, Christy Joy. We decided to compile a top-ten list for keeping a peaceful marriage. That list turned into a seventy-five-page journal that included twenty-five communication and marriage principles Keith and I live by each day—the same principles that make up the foundation of this book. Until that moment we'd never realized that our argument-free marriage was not happenstance but rather the result of putting boundaries and principles in place to keep us from falling into a relationship riddled with strife.

Writing that journal for my sister made me realize that what Keith and I have experienced in our marriage and the principles we've applied could be replicated in others' lives to build solid, healthy, loving, and energized marriages. Since then, we have passed on the principles of a peaceful union to our family, friends, and now you.

IMPORTANT NOTE ABOUT ABUSIVE MARRIAGES

Unfortunately—and it's probably better that I mention this here than wait until you've invested time in reading the following pages—this book is not intended for those in abusive relationships, whether physical or emotional.

Yes, I believe every marriage has redemptive qualities, but when any kind of abuse is involved in the relationship, you should seek professional help without delay. The principles and strategies I will outline in the pages that will follow are for spouses who are interested in learning how to create an argument-free marriage— but who already have an abuse-free one.

SHOULD YOUR GOAL BE AN "ARGUMENT-FREE" OR "ARGUE-LESS" MARRIAGE?

Understanding so many people would find the concept of an argument-free marriage difficult, this book nearly went to print with a different name: *Argue Less, Love More.* I was concerned about the negative things people might say, and my goal is always to encourage positivity, happiness, laughter, and all those things that make life so beautiful. The day before this manuscript was due to the publisher, I changed the name back.

Many people have written about, and will continue to write about, how to argue less in marriage. But my heart's desire is for you to know arguments aren't necessary at all. And I believe every marriage, if *you* (and your spouse) so choose, has the ability to be completely free of arguments. As the saying goes, "Say what you mean; just don't say it mean." Setting a goal to have a marriage free of arguments is a lofty but doable one. And if it's in your heart to go for it, this book will give you the tools you need to succeed. If your desire is simply to decrease the number of arguments and increase the love in your marriage, this book will also get you there. Both an "argument-free" and "argue-less" marriage are progress. You decide which one is right for you.

STILL POINT IN A TURNING WORLD

Life can be tough. Curveballs thrown at you from every side. But just as in baseball, the excitement players feel when they've circled all the bases and safely reached home is what I hope you will feel each day when you reach home.

Your home—whether a house, apartment, basement, or wherever you rest your head next to your spouse—should be a refuge from the outside world, where guards and walls come down and you are free to be the person you were created to be. A place where love and laughter abound.

Years ago I lived in a community where every home had a name. Although each house had an address, the address plates also included a name the owner thought most befitting. Every day I'd take a short walk through the neighborhood and would stop at one particular home. I can't remember what the house looked like, as that is not what drew my attention. It was its name: *Still Point in a Turning World*. Just reading their address plate was a breath of fresh air. I hoped one day I'd find that. Then I did.

Marriage is the greatest partnership known to man. When you are down, you have a friend by your side to lift you up. The dream that seems unreachable or the challenge that appears insurmountable all of a sudden becomes easier when you have a partner by your side to help you along this sometimes rocky road called life.

Your home is your personal sanctuary. That place you go to be refreshed, renewed, and reinvigorated to take on the world. Your marriage should never drain you but replenish you after the world has taken so much.

When I think about marriage, this is how I view it. Some

may consider it Pollyannaish, but it's the only kind of marriage I've personally experienced and it is one I hope you now—or will one day soon—enjoy for yourself. Because as Ronald Reagan once said about his wife, "There is no greater happiness for a man than approaching a door at the end of the day and knowing someone on the other side of that door is waiting for the sound of his footsteps." That is exactly how I feel when I come home and my husband has arrived before me and vice versa.

If what I've described above is not how you feel about your marriage, then this book is most assuredly for you. Test the principles in this book for the next twenty-eight days. If you and your spouse commit to giving these principles a trial run, I'm confident you will discover that you are holding the keys that unlock the secret to revolutionizing and reenergizing your relationship.

Are you ready to create an argument-free (or at the very least, an "argue-less") marriage? Then let's roll!

Week One

THE PLAN FOR A
HARMONIOUS MARRIAGE

IF THIS DRIVEWAY COULD SPEAK, IT WOULD TELL OF THE day Tim and Renee stood at the top of the winding pavement and said good-bye to each other. Tim helped lift the last of Renee's bags into her car as tears streamed down their faces.

They'd been married for less than a year. Their fairy-tale wedding had been the talk of the town. Guests at the posh Beverly Hills reception spent the evening toasting the dashing groom and his young bride in a ballroom that had seen its share of weddings come and go. And nearly as fast as the ceremony, in the blink of an eye, the marriage was over. Kaput.

Tim and Renee had both determined the marriage wasn't worth all the arguing, fighting, and distrust that had resulted from their actions. They'd gone against the advice of friends and family in deciding to be married, and shortly after the ceremony they concluded everyone else was right.

The wedding had been beautiful. The marriage, not so much.

THE NEWLYWED MYTH

I don't know of one couple who married hoping they would one day divorce. Do you?

Yet we've heard for decades that the divorce rate in the United States is approximately 50 percent. And although that number has been disputed for just about as long as it's been stated, what we know is roughly one out of every two couples who pledge, "For better or worse, for richer, for poorer, in sickness and in health," don't keep that vow to each other.

What most people don't realize is that the highest percentage of marriages that dissolve end within the first five years. Worldwide, divorces peak in the fourth year.[1]

As it turns out, the so-called newlywed years are a total farce. Couples are told the first years will be the easiest, so they go into marriage with that expectation in mind. And when difficulties come much earlier than anticipated, many think, *If these are the easy years, then I'm not sticking around for the tough ones!* They don't stop to consider that the coming together of two hearts, two souls, and two independent spirits is a lifelong work, not something to be completed in a matter of months.

Two people fell in love based on their similarities, only to determine later that their differences were insurmountable. If only they knew, while repeating their vows, that sometimes the "worse" happens before the "better." In fact, for married couples who make it through their first four years, the divorce rate begins to decrease after their five-year anniversary and then dips significantly after the tenth year of marriage.[2]

Marriage is risky business, but the rewards are worth the risk. In 1870, in a letter to Queen Victoria's fourth daughter upon the announcement of her engagement, British prime minister

Benjamin Disraeli wrote, "There is no greater risk than matrimony. But there is nothing happier than a happy marriage."

Disraeli pinpointed why we continue to place bets on this horse that seems to only have a fifty-fifty chance of winning. We hope to fall on the side of marriages that are a good investment and, with maturity and growth, reap favorable returns.

At the heart of it all, we are dreamers. Even the most pessimistic or pragmatic person will probably concede that it takes some level of faith and an ability to dream to believe in a romance and love that can last a lifetime. Yet marriages like that begin each and every day, and many of them last fifty, sixty, or even seventy glorious years, ending not through divorce but through the passing of a spouse.

WHY DID YOU CHOOSE YOUR SPOUSE?

For the past eleven years, I've had the great pleasure of being a part of something that is rarely seen on television, in the movies, or in the media overall: a happy marriage. I pinch myself daily that I wake up next to my favorite person on earth. Truly. And since founding an online club for married women in 2010, I've had the fortune of interacting with millions of women who feel the same way I do about their spouses.

Whatever caused you to fall in love and say "I do" is probably what also motivated you to read this book. You and I still believe in the power of love and the joy and peace marriage has to offer if we'll just put in the effort to make it great.

Some of you might say, "But you don't know my spouse. Maybe your husband is not as frustrating as mine." I will tell you the same thing my mother used to tell women who complained to her about their mates: "I don't know your husband, and he may be as irrational as you claim. But what I do know is you had a choice. And *you* chose him."

What made you choose your spouse? Out of the seven billion people in the world, what was so special about him or her that caused you to forsake all others? Let's begin here. And for two minutes, let's pause here. I urge you to think about this question as you begin this challenge, as it will guide you to a more fulfilling journey.

Unfortunately, many people have chosen a poor mate. That is indeed a challenge. But there is hope. If your spouse is willing to take this twenty-eight-day challenge with you and is not abusive physically or emotionally (see my note about this in the introduction), I believe by the end of day twenty-eight, your relationship will be stronger, more loving, and harmonious.

THE ROAD TO DIVORCE IS
PAVED WITH ARGUMENTS

If you've ever been around a couple contemplating divorce, you probably know three of the top reasons cited for dissolutions: poor communication, growing apart, and stress caused by financial difficulties. Narrowing down the top reasons for divorce statistically yields some interesting results. For every study released claiming to know the "top three reasons for divorce," another is released with different findings. What we know for certain is the vast majority of divorces are preceded by years of arguing.

No one gets married hoping one day the marriage will fall apart (at least no one I've ever met). But life happens, and those small things many spouses were once willing to overlook—quirks, idiosyncrasies, imperfections, failures—all of a sudden become the main focus. A world full of broken, jaded, and hardened hearts is a dangerous world to live in. Life in a place where broken homes are the majority is a disheartening existence. But *you* can help change that. You already have by picking up this book and taking up this twenty-eight-day challenge.

No one truly knows how a couple progresses from seemingly unimportant arguments to divorce court, but what we do know is one often leads to another. In most cases it is not the disagreements themselves but rather how we handle and resolve such conflicts that determine the ultimate outcome.

The plan for an argument-free marriage is simple: stop the arguments, and then restore, revive, and reenergize the intimacy in your relationship. As you and your spouse learn how to implement that plan through this twenty-eight-day challenge, you will realize that the answer to the question, How in the world do two people with different thoughts, beliefs, and personalities coexist and not argue? is simpler than you may think.

───────── *Day One Challenge Questions* ─────────

1. What made you choose your spouse? Jot down a few of your spouse's characteristics that were appealing to you.
2. Describe your "newlywed years" of marriage. In what ways did your marriage meet your expectations in those early years? In what ways was your new marriage different from how you had imagined it would be?
3. How would your relationship with your spouse be different if you didn't argue? How would an argument-free marriage affect your children? Your family? Your own life? Be specific.

What Most Arguments
Are Really About

At the time I began writing this book, I was the general manager of a bustling hotel, and Keith was a senior executive of a Fortune 500 company. Every day when we came home we were absolutely pooped. We ended our days with little to no energy, and by the time we walked through the door of our home, we just wanted to head to bed and go right to sleep. All our vigor had been drained. But at the sight of each other, the weight of the world was lifted off our shoulders, our energy reappeared, and we took a deep breath. *Ahhh* . . . life is good.

Several years into our marriage we learned that most of our married friends have the opposite reaction. After a long and tiring day, they come home and are on edge. They are easily irritated, and the simplest thing can set off an argument that will last an hour, a day, and in some cases up to a week. Keith and I had never really considered the differences between these reactions and ours until a reporter from the *Los Angeles Times* conducted an interview with me.

The reporter was writing an article about an online club I

founded called the Happy Wives Club (HappyWivesClub.com). I was fed up with all the cynicism about marriage being played out on the big screen, on television, and in magazines, and I'd decided to do something about it. My interview with the *Times* lasted two hours and probed my life, marriage, husband, and viewpoints on a vast range of marriage-related topics, including the best way to resolve an argument.

The seasoned journalist looked baffled when I shared that Keith and I had never had an argument. Her expression conveyed disbelief. And who could fault her? Then came the questions. It was her reaction—and the reaction of those who have responded to our argument-free marriage with, "Well, what do you consider to be an argument?"—that underscored my desire to write this book.

WHAT IS AN ARGUMENT?

Maybe the most helpful thing as you begin your journey to an argument-free marriage is to first understand what I define as an argument. The definition I most often use is the same one that will appear at the top of your screen if you type the term into Google: "an exchange of diverging or opposite views, typically a heated or angry one."

It is the latter portion of that definition that I truly believe can be avoided. Having a "heated or angry" exchange is the opposite of sharing your opposing views with each other in a way that allows you to have a meaningful discussion that yields positive results (even if the result is to agree to disagree, something Keith and I have done many times over the years). The best description

I've seen of the differences between an argument and a discussion was posted by William Jones on the Good Enough Mother site and republished on my own site:

1. A discussion = People take turns really listening to each other.
2. An argument = Everyone's talking; nobody's listening.
3. A discussion = Two people against a problem.
4. An argument = Two people against each other.
5. A discussion = Is about the situation at hand.
6. An argument = Is seldom actually about the thing being argued over.
7. A discussion = Is about an important issue.
8. An argument = Is seldom about anything except who's right and who's wrong.
9. A discussion = There are millions of good reasons to have one.
10. An argument = There is NO good reason to have one.
11. A discussion = Can solve a problem.
12. An argument = Never really solves anything.
13. A discussion = Ends when people agree on a solution.
14. An argument = Doesn't end; it just waits to be brought up in the next argument.
15. A discussion = The people who solve the problem win.
16. An argument = Nobody wins.

When an argument is elevated to finger-pointing, throwing things, or otherwise using anything other than your words, I consider that a fight. I include this statement because I've seen so much about the difference between an argument and a fight in marriage that I wanted to clarify how I view both. I also define a *fight* the same way Google does: "a violent struggle involving the exchange of physical blows or the use of weapons." In many instances, a conflict does not come to actual blows, but the words exchanged are elevated to such a hurtful nature that it's hard to distinguish between an argument and a fight.

LASTING CONSEQUENCES OF ARGUMENTS

Driving down the 405 freeway not long ago, I experienced what is common on the streets and highways of Los Angeles: midday traffic. But I also had a new experience, one I will not soon forget. Out of the corner of my eye, I saw a large, black Mercedes with a young girl sitting to the far-right side of the backseat. She caught my eye because she sat slouched with her head down, almost as if she wished she could simply disappear. A black jacket hood covered most of her face, although it was not cold outside.

As I pulled up a little more, I could see why this girl was attempting to fade into the background. A couple, presumably her parents, sat in the front seat. Dad was behind the wheel while Mom sat in the passenger seat, yelling and waving her index finger—at Dad. Both took turns yelling and pointing at each other. And with every passing second, I watched the girl shrink away more and more.

I was heartbroken for the little girl. I wanted to pull up beside their car, roll down my window, and plead with her parents, "Can't you figure out a better way to communicate in front of your daughter? Do you have any idea what your argument is doing to her?" I wished I could have given the girl some words of comfort. But they passed me before I could even get close enough to smile at her.

My heart was saddened. I felt for the little girl as I watched her car drive away. Later that day I continued to think about her. I wondered if her parents argued like that in front of her all the time or if it was just an off day for them. Then I imagined what it must feel like to be a child living with parents who constantly choose to use harsh, angry words with each other. (Sadly, some of you reading this don't have to imagine that because you lived through it.) I pictured the tears she must cry in the dark of night when no one is around. I thought of the poor communication skills she was learning that would undoubtedly find their way into her classroom, friendships, and, later in life, her workplace and possibly her own marriage.

I truly believe that fighting and arguments may be helpful in war or in the courtroom, but not in the home. They may help your cause when you are opposing the person on the other side. But not when you are a team. And in marriage, you are a team. For this reason I will not waver on this belief: a marriage can be full of passion, with spouses completely honest and transparent with each other, and not involve arguing. I believe this because when it comes to arguments in marriage, they very rarely help. But they consistently and almost always hurt.

What Causes Arguments?

When you think about it, what really causes arguments? (I'm talking about arguments here, not disagreements.) The cause of most arguments boils down to one thing: our own self-interests.

They come from our self-seeking desires that battle within us. We want what we want, when we want it, how we want it, period. I know my next statement might elicit protests, but arguments are never *really* about what our spouses did or said. They stem from our own expectations of what our spouses should have done or could have said instead.

It is human nature to think, *It's all about me.* Once a month I get together with two of my closest girlfriends and have what we call our "ladies' night." Our hubbies get out of Dodge as we fill the house with a nice dose of estrogen. Recently we finished reading the book *It's Not About Me* by Max Lucado. Writing about human nature, Lucado says,

> Self-promotion. Self-preservation. Self-centeredness. It's all about me!
>
> They all told us it was, didn't they? Weren't we urged to look out for number one? Find our place in the sun? Make a name for ourselves? We thought self-celebration would make us happy. . . .
>
> But what chaos this philosophy creates. What if a symphony orchestra followed such an approach? Can you imagine an orchestra with an "It's all about me" outlook? Each artist clamoring for self-expression. Tubas blasting nonstop. Percussionists pounding to get attention. The cellist shoving the flutist out of the center-stage chair. The trumpeter standing atop the conductor's stool tooting his horn. Sheet music disregarded. Conductor ignored. What do you have but an endless tune-up session![1]

Isn't this the way we go through life? Believing everything is about us? Believing our spouses are here solely to take care of us and make us happy? In a relationship where we should be making beautiful music together, we are banging away on our drums, demanding to be heard, demanding to be right.

Ego. Selfishness. The desire to be right. Aren't these really, truly the root of most arguments and quarrels in marriage? Add to these factors our lack of patience and our need for instant gratification. We need an answer now! We deserve a response now! Me! Me! *Me!*

The impatience you often display when arguing with your spouse is not too dissimilar from what young children do when they are on a long car ride to an amusement park or some other place they'd rather be. "Are we there yet? Are we there yet? Are we there yet?" At fifteen minutes into a two-hour trip, the parent finds the questions amusing. The pestering gets less entertaining by the third or fourth time the question is posed. Then come the squirminess, fussiness, and occasional crying until Mom or Dad finally says, "No! I'll tell you when we get there."

You want what you want, and your spouse wants what he or she wants. Arguing will cause you both to go without your hearts' desires. You may win the argument and get your way, but at what expense? Think about some of your silliest arguments with your spouse. A toilet seat left up. A remote control misplaced. Clothes left around the house. The kids weren't picked up from school on time. A meeting at the office ran late, which meant that dinner with the kids didn't start promptly at six thirty.

Whatever the argument, was it worth it? How many hurtful things did you say to your spouse? Was the pain you inflicted worth the temporary satisfaction you received? Did your spouse's minor infraction or momentary insensitivity warrant your angry response?

Is "Winning" Worth the Wounds?

Years ago I read a story about a young boy with a bad temper. Handing his son a bag of nails, the boy's father explained that each time his son lost his temper and shouted angry, hurtful words, he must hammer a nail into the back of the wooden fence in their yard. On that first day, thirty-seven nails went into the fence. During the next few weeks, the boy began discovering it was easier to hold his temper and his tongue than trek all the way out to the back and pound those nails into the fence.

After some time, the boy proudly approached his father and announced he had not lost his temper at all for several days. The wise father suggested his son pull out one nail for each temper-free day. Finally, boasting that all the nails were gone, the boy took his dad's hand and led him to the fence without nails. The father said, "You have done well, my son. Now look at the holes in the fence. It will never be the same. When you say things in anger, your words leave scars, just like these holes."

How many wounds have you left on your spouse, not physically but emotionally, because of your unkind words in the heat of an argument? He or she may continue moving forward, but harmful words and actions never completely fade. Even if your spouse has fully forgiven you, he or she is not God. Husbands and wives may forgive, but chances are they will not forget, no matter how hard they try.

At what point will you decide that winning an argument is not worth the hurt caused to your spouse or the damage created to the "fence" of your marriage? How about today? How about right now? At this moment you can do it. All you need is patience and a desire to have a loving and intimate relationship for the remaining days of your life.

Such patience comes when you make the decision "for richer, for poorer, in sickness and in health, to love and to cherish, till death do us part." When you and your spouse determine you have the rest of your lives to resolve an issue, you remove the requirement of coming to an agreement right then, right there. Some emergencies need to be addressed immediately, but most can be worked out over time.

————— *Day Two Challenge Questions* —————

1. Think back to your most recent argument with your spouse. What was it about? Now think a little deeper— what was that argument really about? Did your ego, pride, self-interest, or even past pain play a role in your reaction? Explain.
2. Who "won" the most recent argument: you or your spouse? What was the cost of "winning" in terms of your relationship, your family, and your intimacy with each other?
3. "You have the rest of your lives to resolve an issue." How does this long-term mind-set affect your perspective on your most recent argument with your spouse? Is the issue you argued about significant in the big picture of a lifetime together?

THROW OUT YOUR PLAN B

FOR MANY YEARS, ACTOR WILL SMITH HAS BEEN CONSIDERED one of the most bankable movie stars in the world. The term *bankable* is used in the movie industry when referencing a person—actor, producer, director, and so on—with guaranteed success at the box office. For the past fifteen or so years, no one has done better than Will Smith. Of the sixteen movies released in his career, only three have not performed well. And of those three "failures," one received two Oscar nominations.

Smith has acted in movies in nearly every genre—romance, comedy, drama, and sci-fi—and has succeeded in every category. He is the only actor to date to have eight consecutive films gross over $100 million. He's also had eight consecutive number one box-office spots. His movies have grossed over $6.6 billion worldwide. This actor holds the record for highest average gross per film, in history, in the world.

One might attribute Smith's success to his talent, hard work, infectious personality, and kindness. But while people within the entertainment industry acknowledge those characteristics, he possesses an even more important quality. What is his secret to success in business? Well, it's not much of a secret because he's shared it with nearly every interviewer who has posed this question throughout his career: he has no plan B.

Early in life, Smith says, his father taught him a valuable lesson: "Have no plan B. It distracts from plan A." These words of wisdom have brought him to where he is today in the entertainment industry. This philosophy allowed him to stay focused on his goal of success. In a *Time* magazine article, he said, "Even contemplating a plan B, you almost create the necessity for a plan B."[1]

Having no plan B is extremely smart on many levels, and "no plan B" is the ideal mantra for marriage. If you enter a situation with a backup plan in mind, it generally means you are spending some time and energy on not being successful. While there are circumstances in life where this is a sound approach, it is never sound in marriage.

When you know you will be together for a lifetime, you don't store up negative feelings or issues. When you are not planning for anything in life that doesn't include your spouse, you can truly be focused solely on the success of your plan A.

A SECRET OF HAPPY
MARRIAGES—NO PLAN B

Over the years I've interviewed many couples, and in my debut book, *Happy Wives Club*, I shared my discovery of the twelve common denominators ("secrets," if you will) among couples with the most loving, kind, patient, and lasting relationships. One common denominator: they have no plan B. No matter what, divorce and infidelity are not an option. For this reason arguments are few, if any, because they know they have a lifetime to come to an agreement. A meeting of the minds need not occur in *every* conversation because they know they have time to work it out.

Life is full of various stresses. But during the tough times, couples with no plan B dig their heels into the sand and commit to work through challenges *together*, no matter how difficult the decisions facing them are.

My friends Elijah and Simone have been married more than thirty years. Throughout most of their marriage, Elijah's successful restaurant allowed Simone to be a stay-at-home mom. Then the nationwide economic crisis of 2009 struck, and far fewer people were dining at upscale restaurants like the one Elijah owned.

As a result, their debt began to mount, and as difficult as it was for Simone to send out résumés for the first time in three decades, she knew her husband needed her help. She didn't complain or whine. She didn't make him feel bad for not being able to take care of the family. She encouraged him and said, "We're in this together, baby."

Elijah and Simone always believed everything would work out in the end as long as they were willing to give their all to their relationship. That is what happens when a couple decides to have no plan B. Forgiveness is par for the course, ego is thrown to the wind, and complete dedication and surrender—on the part of both husband and wife—is strived for unceasingly.

If plan A is a happy, healthy, and successful marriage, and you and your spouse remain laser-beam focused on that, then you will invest the time necessary to ensure its success. Nothing and no one will be able to come between you or cause you to waver in your determination, because failure is not an option. Alternatively, a plan B subconsciously drains the heart, soul, and effort poured into a marriage. Why should anyone give every ounce of his or her being to a relationship that might not last?

There are many principles to creating, nurturing, and enjoying an argument-free marriage, but at the very top of the list is having no backup or "just in case" plans. When couples stand before God, family, and friends and pledge to stay together "till death do us part," they are making a solid commitment to each other until the end of their lives.

THE FREEDOM OF FREELY GIVING ALL

With an active community of close to one million married women on Facebook (Facebook.com/happywivesclub), I often post questions there for the women happily married for twenty-five or more years. I ask them to share their advice with newlyweds so they can create the best marriage possible from the very start. These are women with no plan B. You can see it in their responses every time, and they usually include the words: "Never give up!"

Do you have any plan Bs? Any "just in case" thoughts that roam through your mind? Any bank accounts your spouse doesn't know about? Do you talk with friends about what life would be like if you were still single? Do you fantasize about whom you might be with if you weren't married to your current spouse? Have you thought about how much money you'd need to earn in order to take care of yourself should your marriage come to an end?

We live in a society of plan Bs. When Keith and I married, I took his last name and urged him to merge and manage our finances. We make joint decisions on all important matters, including our finances, but he's the financial manager in our family. He enjoys that sort of thing. As a former hotel general manager and restaurant business manager who spent more time looking at profit and loss statements than doing anything else, I assure you, I didn't mind handing over the day-to-day financial management.

Judging by some of the comments I have received about these decisions, you would have thought I had destroyed the feminist movement in that single act. It's almost as if people thought I was a throwback to the wives of the 1950s. I assure you I'm no June Cleaver. But I have always taken my vows seriously, and I give my whole heart to this love and our relationship.

Making a decision to freely give my all has provided me with more freedom than any wife I know, except for others who have made the same decision. I do not live in fear that my husband will one day cheat or leave me. That may seem naïve, but I believe my attitude reflects courage and strength. I am not concerned about the future. I'm loving life, my marriage, and my husband to the fullest without any worry, fear, or concern.

If you are not ready to destroy thoughts or activities related to a plan B, this book is not for you at this time. I do not believe an argument-free marriage is possible in the absence of this foundational principle.

A JOINT COMMITMENT TO PLAN A

For many of you reading this, you might be trying to figure out how to stop the fussing and fighting, but your spouse might think there's nothing wrong with that communication style. I wish I could tell you this twenty-eight-day challenge will work just through your desire to make it happen. But unfortunately, that is not the case. Both you and your spouse must desire an argument-free marriage for this twenty-eight-day challenge to work. You must both be on the same page in desiring a stronger, kinder, and more loving relationship.

If you and your spouse are up for the challenge and ready to set aside the misconception that marriage and arguments must go hand in hand, here's what I ask you to do: spend the next few days getting rid of anything related to a plan B or destroying any practice that might lead to one.

You'd be surprised at how many marriages have been destroyed by something as simple as staying in touch with an old flame via Facebook. You might be thinking, *Well, what am I supposed to do? Unfriend them?* Yes! Absolutely! And as quickly as possible. You may not realize how swiftly this "harmless" relationship can become a plan B, but ask around and you'll quickly discover this has been the precursor to more divorces than we can even count. It's simply not worth risking a lifelong relationship of love and commitment for the friendship of an ex-flame.

There are numerous Facebook-type backup plans that many hold dear. I'd recommend not moving on to the next chapter until you and your spouse have truly resolved to have no plan B. The reason is simple: it distracts from plan A.

—————— *Day Three Challenge Questions* ——————

1. Do you have any plan Bs? Any "just in case" thoughts? Examples include things like a private bank account, fantasies of being with someone other than your spouse, or thoughts of how much money you'd need to support yourself if your marriage ends. Think about all the things that could quickly turn into plan Bs if you aren't careful.

2. Think through any plan Bs you may have considered in question one. Are you ready to destroy all thoughts and activities related to your plan Bs? If so, think about the specific steps you will take to make those changes (such as closing a private bank account, unfriending ex-flames on Facebook, etc.). Talk with your spouse and express your commitment to focus solely on plan A from now on. Remember, you and your spouse must be on the same page for this twenty-eight-day challenge to work.

3. In what areas are you holding back from your spouse—not "freely giving all"? Starting today, what changes can you make to become completely open and committed in all areas of your marriage?

STOP ACCELERATION BEFORE IT STARTS

THE SPEED OF MY FEET WAS NO MATCH FOR THE FLOOD OF thoughts rushing through my mind as I walked quickly up and down the residential hills of Westlake Village and Thousand Oaks. How dare he do that? After I opened my heart and our home so his parents could be comfortable, how could he be so thoughtless?

It had only been a few months since Keith's parents moved into our house. I love Mom and Pop and consider them my "bonus" parents. They were in the process of looking for a new home closer to the community in which we lived. At the time, Keith and I had just begun seriously talking about having children. His mom had just retired, and his pop (what we call Keith's stepdad) would be retiring less than a year later. We knew his mom's desire was to live close to the grandchildren, and you can't get much closer than in the same house.

While driving home from a professional volleyball match in Manhattan Beach, I received a call from Keith. "Sweetheart, Mom and Pop are thinking about moving close by, and I wanted to get your thoughts. It doesn't make sense for them to live so far away when they're going to want to visit their grandbabies several times a week." He was calling to get my opinion on a community adjacent to where we live. He hadn't even finished the question before I suggested they move in with us.

The next day we told Mom and Pop we wanted to come by their home to talk with them. As soon as we sat down together, Keith and I offered to let them move in with us. We had more than enough room—too much room, really—and were hardly ever home. We worked such long hours that we were rarely able to enjoy our house in the daylight. With Mom and Pop moving in, someone would finally be able to enjoy our beautiful home, which we had affectionately named Serenity Ranch, for more than a few waking hours a day.

When we extended the invitation, I had two requests. The first was that Pop not start any home-improvement projects. I loved our home just the way it was and didn't want any changes made. Keith and Pop are both do-it-yourself home-improvement men, and I wanted to make sure that when I came home at the end of a busy day, everything would be the same way, structurally and aesthetically, that I had left it in the morning. The second, and to me the more important request, was that they not keep any junk food or sweets in the house.

In my early twenties I was overweight. The extra weight simply dragged me down. I spent six months slowly getting the weight off and had maintained the loss for more than ten years by the time Keith's parents moved in with us. One of the bedrocks of my weight-loss success was that I did not keep junk food or sweets in the house. I love sweets, any kind of sweets! It was critical that if I wanted to have some, I'd need to leave the house to get them.

Needless to say, when I made this request of Keith's parents,

I expected it to be honored. Unfortunately, neither his parents nor Keith fully understood the seriousness of this request and thus were not mindful of it. Maybe I did not communicate well enough, or possibly it seemed so insignificant that they didn't think much about it. After all, I was disciplined in my eating and had not been overweight the entire time they'd known me, so they might have concluded it was no big deal—until the day I nearly blew a gasket.

A few months into our new living arrangement, and a few years into our marriage, I woke up one morning and just about hit the ceiling. Throughout most of the night, the aroma of freshly baked pies had wafted through the air-conditioning vent of our bedroom. I couldn't sleep because my sweet-loving body thought it was time to wake up and eat. When I got out of bed, I went in the kitchen and discovered homemade pies all over the center island. I could feel the anger rising inside of me.

I went to Keith and exclaimed, "This isn't right! I have done everything I can to make them comfortable, and I've made only two requests." My frustration was directed at Keith because I'd asked him to address the "sweets and junk food in the house" issue on several occasions, and he had never followed through.

I knew if I continued this conversation, I would be embarking upon the first argument ever with my loving husband. As quickly as possible, I put on my tennis shoes and began to walk. I decided I would continue walking until all the angry voices in my head quieted down, and I could think and communicate my feelings to Keith fairly and reasonably. Those voices became louder and louder, telling me I was right and Keith and his parents were being unfair. *You have every right to be mad right now!* one voice said. *You should call Keith and give him a piece of your mind!* another one jabbed.

THE LAW OF ACCELERATION

What was going on at that moment was an example of what I call the law of acceleration (not to be confused with Newton's laws of motion). In early 2010, Japanese automaker Toyota found itself in a lot of hot water. A defect in its cars had caused several models to accelerate even while the driver was pressing on the brakes. In a *Los Angeles Times* article on March 10, 2010, a driver recounted his tale of how he sped up on the freeway to pass another car, and when he attempted to slow down by applying the brakes, the car kept increasing in speed.

For thirty miles, this driver swerved in and out of traffic, pounding on his brakes, at one point narrowly missing a big rig. Finally, a police officer responding to the driver's 911 call pulled up beside him and instructed him to hold down the brakes with his full might while engaging the emergency brake. These actions slowed the car to fifty miles per hour, allowing him to finally turn off the ignition and coast to safety.

What this driver described happening to his Toyota is what so often happens to us when a spouse hurts, disappoints, or saddens us. Rather than paying attention to that original emotion, that place of vulnerability, we allow the voices in our heads to cause us to accelerate. When we zoom ahead, we go from hurt to angry, from disappointed to frustrated, and from sad to mad. I'll discuss these original emotions in more detail in the next chapter.

On the day of the "pie incident," I understood the law of acceleration and knew if I didn't get out of the house—right then, right there—I was going to lose control. So I kept walking. And walking. And walking.

I walked for six hours before returning home. Somewhere

around the second hour of this walk, the voices began to subside. I became calm enough to leave Keith a voice message letting him know where I'd gone. Now, I don't recommend you leave without telling your spouse where you are going. But my husband knows me so well he would have known how to trace my steps if necessary. I also made sure to walk down a path familiar to both of us. (By the way, I realize that most of you don't have six hours to walk off your anger—and if it hadn't happened on a weekend, I wouldn't have either! The point of my story isn't how long I walked, but rather that I took some time away from the situation to calm down and sort through my thoughts and feelings.)

By the time I returned home, I'd silenced the voices and was ready to talk to Keith. I calmly told him how much it hurt my feelings that he'd chosen to side with his parents (at least that is what his behavior seemed like at the time) by not putting his foot down on this one issue.

We talked about it. I expressed why I was hurt, and he expressed the uncomfortable position he had been placed in. He hadn't yet figured out the best way to handle the conflict between my desires and his parents'. (I told you he was the diplomat of the family.) He saw my side, and I saw his. We decided not to say anything to Mom and Pop so they could continue feeling comfortable in their new home. Instead, we designated a "sweets and junk-food cabinet," and I simply stayed out of it. Today we all laugh. The junk-food cabinet is pitifully bare, because after living with us for a year, Mom and Pop stopped bringing junk food into the house. They want to eat healthier too.

You might think I lost this battle. But I can tell you the outcome was completely worth the loss. I gained insight into the relationship between Keith's mom and her only child, as well as a deep understanding of his love and respect for his mom and stepdad. In that moment I was reminded that family life is not always about me.

Keith learned how strong I am, though he also saw that I am willing to compromise on issues that could have triggered a huge fight. He loved and respected me even more by the end of that day, and I hadn't even known that was possible. As soon as Keith saw me, he pulled me into his arms, embraced me, and told me he was sorry. Argument averted. Relationship intact.

WHAT STARTS SMALL QUICKLY GROWS LARGER

After sharing this story on my Happy Wives Club site, I received a flurry of negative comments about how selfish I was as a daughter-in-law or how silly I was for allowing something so small to become so big. The first set of comments about my selfishness didn't take into account that not only did I invite my in-laws to live with us, but I also moved us out of our upstairs master bedroom and into a small guest bedroom off the kitchen.

I had given up my privacy (which is hard for a gal my husband calls "nature girl" because of my fondness for walking around the house in my skivvies) and so much more to ensure they felt welcome and felt like my home was their home. But this request of mine, albeit small and possibly silly, was incredibly important to me, and I had expected them to abide by it.

More important, based on the tone of some of the comments on my site, I concluded that the commenters' blood must have been boiling as they wrote them. So I wondered what their most recent argument with their spouse was about and how "big" the issues were.

In marriage, couples often argue about the little things. Those tiny things pile up into much larger issues, which begin to cause distance and a lack of intimacy. Couples grow apart when partners subconsciously create a distance between each other. What begins small can quickly grow into something much greater. The good news is we can put a stop to the arguments before they have a chance to begin if we truly understand and heed the law of acceleration.

Day Four Challenge Questions

1. Describe a time when the law of acceleration turned a small annoyance into a full-blown argument with your spouse. What factors caused the discussion to accelerate? What were the results?
2. What are some things you can do in the heat of the moment to "cool off" and stop the law of acceleration before it starts? Examples include going for a walk, taking a time-out in another room, working in the garden, taking a relaxing bath or long shower, etc.
3. Ask your spouse what activities he or she would like to do to "cool off" when disagreements become heated. Determine ahead of time that you will graciously honor your spouse's request to take a time-out from a heated discussion if needed. Discuss how becoming familiar with each other's preferred means of calming down can help defuse arguments before they start.

PAY ATTENTION TO THE
ORIGINAL EMOTION

THE SAME YEAR TOYOTA WAS REPAIRING DAMAGE TO ITS image caused by that mechanical acceleration issue, Rosie O'Donnell attempted to make reparations to her image in an interview with Oprah Winfrey. Discussing the huge fight between O'Donnell and iconic journalist Barbara Walters, which resulted in O'Donnell's departure from the Emmy Award–winning show *The View*, Oprah asked, "Do you regret that moment?"

"Yes, I do," O'Donnell responded. She said she regretted using her words as weapons and "scaring" Walters with her out-of-control rage. What O'Donnell said next confounded even the talk-show queen herself: "For me, at that moment, if I had been braver, I would have just cried and said, 'You really hurt my feelings.'"

Oprah clapped her hands as if having one of her famous *aha* moments and said, "That is so interesting! That you would say, 'If I had been braver, I would have just cried.' Because oftentimes crying is perceived as the weak thing to do." She then asked O'Donnell why crying would have been braver than yelling and screaming and saying hurtful words.

O'Donnell's response illustrates the principles in this chapter better than anything I could hope to say. She said, "Because then you're vulnerable. Then the authentic feeling that I had, [which] was pain and hurt and rejection, [would have come out]." Instead, as she told Oprah, she put on the same armor she'd chosen to protect herself since she was a child. She shielded her vulnerability and masked her hurt feelings with anger.[1]

Consider the last time you were in an argument with your spouse. Hold that thought for a brief moment, but don't allow yourself to become angry all over again. Now that you have the thought in your mind, let's talk about the argument. What was the exact thing that set you off? I'm talking about what you felt, not what you discussed. What was your original emotion in that moment? Was it hurt? Fear? Sadness? Disappointment? Insecurity? What portion of your underbelly was exposed?

When we become angry enough to begin arguing, we allow the original emotion, which would expose our vulnerability, to be covered up by a more aggressive, defensive response. Rather than exposing the softer side of ourselves, we put up shields and pull out our verbal swords and begin swinging. We swing left, we swing right, aimlessly out of control and missing the target every time. Yes, we may slice and dice the hearts of our spouses, but we miss the mark because we've not dealt with the true emotion we're feeling.

AVOID ARGUMENTS BY BEING VULNERABLE

Gerald and Kelly moved to California from Kelly's hometown in Nebraska to pursue Gerald's dream of being a radio broadcaster. In the new city Kelly felt like a fish out of water. People didn't speak to her at the grocery store, and she couldn't find any play-dates for her baby girl, Ella. All the women seemed to eat nothing but celery and carrot sticks, while Kelly was a steak-and-potatoes kind of girl. She was miserable in California. She wanted to move back home, where her family and friends lived.

Within a month of moving to the big city, Kelly and Gerald began fighting nonstop. They fought about everything from the amount of groceries she was purchasing (it seemed to Gerald that she was storing up for the winter) to how inconsiderate he was of her feelings. She accused him of not appreciating all the effort she was putting into living in this new city.

Throughout all the arguments, Gerald thought Kelly was just whining, nagging, and complaining. He felt unsupported. Kelly thought Gerald was incapable of understanding how she felt because he got to leave every day and pursue his dream job. Kelly didn't realize that Gerald was scared out of his mind. He feared they'd made a huge mistake and he wouldn't be able to support his family in this big city. So he buried himself in his job, trying to make ends meet. Gerald failed to understand that Kelly was lonely, insecure, and longing for the safety of the world she'd always known.

Gerald was scared. Kelly was lonely. Yet they both covered their vulnerability with anger and insults. This was not their intention. It is simply what seemed to come naturally. Most of us are taught from an early age that arguing is normal. Getting mad is how couples communicate when upset. We are shown how to guard our true feelings and emotions by protecting our hearts. We learn that it's better to go on the offensive than to find ourselves exposed.

The problem with all this is that the behavior leads to blind conversations. Kelly didn't know what Gerald was going through, and Gerald had no clue about Kelly's true feelings. Years later, Keith and I were saddened to hear that this once-loving couple, whose wedding we'd flown to Nebraska to attend, had come to an end. The damage to their marriage during those California years of strife proved to be irreparable.

Paying attention to the original emotion—and thus remaining in a place of vulnerability—is the crux of averting arguments. I realize this is much easier said than done. I am a debater by nature. I grew up arguing and challenging anyone who had an opinion that opposed mine. But for whatever reason, I strove to remain vulnerable with my husband at all times. I still struggle with this principle when it comes to other people, but I don't see that as a bad thing. I don't think vulnerability should be shown to everyone, just to the ones I trust the most, especially my husband.

MOVE FORWARD TOGETHER
WITH YOUR SPOUSE

When transitioning to a relationship of peace and harmony, you need to let your spouse know what you are doing. This is the reason it is so important that both you and your spouse desire an argument-free marriage. I suggest you show your spouse this chapter (as well as the preceding one) to let him or her know that your desire moving forward is to remain at all times in a place of vulnerability in your marriage. Your aim is to pay attention to the original emotion.

Ask your husband or wife to commit to honoring this by protecting your heart—being sensitive to what you are saying and not belittling what may or may not make sense to them—in the moment when you expose your true feelings. Choosing to admit you are hurt rather than declaring you are angry may seem uncomfortable for a moment. It may even sound awkward coming from your mouth, but stick with it. Allow yourself to be completely exposed.

When your spouse puts down the shield of defense and is also vulnerable, do not do anything (laughing, mocking, accusing) that might have an adverse impact on the affection and intimacy of your relationship. Show respect. Don't allow any harm to come to him or her. We must protect our spouses' egos, hearts, emotions, and dreams. This becomes a couple's responsibility the moment they say, "I do."

A NOTE TO HUSBANDS

One of my dearest friends, Taylor, has been married to a wonderful man, Darren, for thirteen years. When Taylor mentioned to her husband one day that Keith and I had never argued, Darren challenged her on that and said it's not possible. The next time the four of us got together, he asked us about it and was shocked when Keith confirmed that we did in fact have an argument-free marriage. We then explained the principle of paying attention to the original emotion. After a half hour of talking about it, Darren was convinced that only Keith and I could succeed in having an argument-free marriage.

The moment I finished the manuscript for this book, I e-mailed a copy to Darren and said, "If there are any holes to be poked in this four-week challenge, I know you'll find them." His response: "I'm happy you're not easily offended, because I plan on poking plenty of holes in your theory!" I knew I was onto something special when he read the manuscript and responded, "There are really no holes to be poked."

There was one area, however, he simply could not wrap his mind around, and that was this notion of paying attention to the original emotion. He couldn't see husbands all around the world telling their wives they wanted to be "vulnerable." He said, "Striving to be vulnerable seems unnatural. Exposed, understanding, unguarded—those words I could probably accept."

I realize that, like Darren, other husbands might find this chapter difficult. So many men are taught never to let their emotions show. They are told it's their responsibility to make sure their wives always feel safe and protected, so they can't show a side of them that is unprotected. But if a man truly desires to create an argument-free marriage, he can and he should. Mutual vulnerability allows both husband and wife to lay it all out on the table. Dreams, hopes, ambitions, fears, hurt—nothing is off-limits.

BRAVE ENOUGH TO BE VULNERABLE

We can't keep everything bottled up inside. We all need to have at least one person we can be completely honest with about our perceived failures, hurts, successes, and hopes. We need to have at least one person who will love and respect us unconditionally. Who better than your spouse to be that person? Who better than the one who shares your bed at night to share your deepest desires with?

As Rosie O'Donnell reminded us through her uncontrolled rage that fateful day in Barbara Walters's dressing room, there is great wisdom in paying attention to the original emotion if we can just be brave enough to be vulnerable.

———— *Day Five Challenge Questions* ————

1. Think back to the last argument you had with your spouse. What was the exact thing that set you off? Not the event—but the emotion. What did you initially feel in that moment? Hurt? Fear? Disappointment? Insecurity? Pay attention to that original emotion and write it down.

2. In your marriage, have you been trying to protect your heart by masking vulnerability with anger and insults? In what ways have you been going on the offensive with your spouse rather than allowing yourself to be exposed? Give specific examples. What do you hope to gain from guarding your heart in these ways? Is this technique helping or hurting your marriage? What do you think would happen if you put down your shield of defense and exposed your true feelings to your spouse? How would that affect your relationship? Could the risk be worth the reward?

3. Consider your latest argument from your spouse's perspective. Is it possible that he or she was masking vulnerability with harsh or angry words? If so, did any of your reactions (laughing, mocking, accusing) at the time reinforce your spouse's fear of being vulnerable with you? Communicate to your spouse that from now on you will show respect and protect his or her heart when your spouse lets down his or her guard with you. Ask your spouse to honor you by protecting your heart when you expose your true feelings.

TIMING IS EVERYTHING

I RECEIVED AN E-MAIL FROM A WOMAN SEEKING ADVICE ON reducing arguments in her relationship. In my response, I explained what Keith has shared on this topic with so many people in the past. Make up your mind to resolve all issues and challenges before the end of the day. For whatever cannot be resolved, either agree to disagree, forgive each other and let it go, or write up a new "work order" for the next day.

DON'T LET THE SUN SET ON YOUR ANGER

Before we set our wedding date, a clinical psychologist who specialized in marriage and family therapy counseled us. He said many things that have stayed with us throughout our marriage, but one of the most important was: "Never let the sun go down while you are angry." This is a proverb our premarital counselor did not expect us to take literally but rather interpreted this as not going to bed angry with each other.

Unfortunately, many couples allow challenges and issues to become exacerbated. Issue A is compounded into issue B, and issue B is attached to issue C. By the time an argument begins, you think you're arguing solely about issue C, but it's really a culmination of all three challenges, which were thrown into a pot and brought to a boil.

The day I got upset with Keith over his parents' junk food in the house was a tough day for me. I knew that when I finally reached home, we needed to talk about why I got so upset. Though I had walked for much longer than I'd ever recommend, I still needed to help Keith understand what hurt me so much. If I didn't address the issue, something similar would probably happen again. Even worse, if I chose to keep the hurt buried inside rather than being open and honest, the issue could have escalated into a huge problem. The next time Keith did something I thought to be inconsiderate, the junk-food issue would have compounded the situation. A molehill quickly becomes a mountain if we allow problems to continue mounting.

In addition to advising we not take our anger to bed with us, the psychologist suggested we have tough conversations only when we are both in our most rational state—not when we are tired and probably will not respond in the wisest or most patient manner. The proverb of never allowing the sun to go down on a difficult conversation, coupled with the simple principle of having weighty conversations before 10:00 p.m., has kept Keith and me from going down paths we would later regret. Whenever we have a difficult discussion, we are able to honestly say what is on our hearts in a way that the other person will be able to receive and understand.

WHEN RESOLUTIONS NEED MORE TIME

Sometimes, however, resolutions need more time. As the general manager of a hotel, I was often frustrated after learning that a problem reported to the engineering department had not yet been fixed. The protocol was that any employee who reported a problem to engineering must write a work order. Once the problem had been fixed, the engineer would write "completed" on the work order and leave a copy in the office. Some work orders, however, remained outstanding for weeks and even months at busy times.

To alleviate this problem, I instituted a new policy. All work orders must be addressed by the end of an engineer's shift. Any work order not completed by the end of the day must have a note stating why the job wasn't completed, plus the name of the engineer to whom the work request was being forwarded. That work order would be closed out and a brand-new work order would be created for the next shift. This was certainly not the most ideal arrangement, as it required more paperwork and additional time to complete the task. But since the original system didn't work, I had to come up with a system that created accountability.

There are times when the issues facing you are more complex than your husband forgetting your daughter's ballet recital or your wife wanting you to be more considerate when you come into the house and not head straight to the couch to watch *SportsCenter*. Sometimes challenges cannot be resolved before the end of the day. These are the times when you agree to let everything go for the evening—and write a work order for the next day. The purpose of this is not to give you a full eight hours to brew in your own anger, but to allow you to get some rest so you can talk about the problem when you are both in your best state of mind (which is usually not at the end of a ten-hour workday).

DISCUSS THE PROBLEM IN YOUR
BEST STATE OF MIND

Here's an example of how this works in our home. Keith has always joked with me about my "sensitive ecosystem." If I drink coffee, my face breaks out the next day. Eating within three hours of my bedtime causes me to have difficulty sleeping and brings on odd dreams. Not getting enough rest causes my eyes to be puffy. I'm sensitive to fragrances and easily get motion sickness on planes, in cars, on amusement-park rides, and quite frankly in anything moving in which I don't have full control.

I could drink milk and eat dairy without a problem until I was thirty, when I became lactose intolerant, with the exception of yogurt and cheese. I wish I could say this is the extent of the list, but I also have an allergy to all things soy, including vegetable oil and soy lecithin, making it pretty tricky to eat out at new restaurants. I am allergic to chocolate and pork, including the lard used in most Mexican food restaurants.

I have no difficulty managing all these issues myself, but it can be challenging for someone like Keith to keep up with. I'm not dramatic about them, because they just are what they are. Before discovering these were all allergies I'd developed as an adult while traveling to different parts of the world, Keith had a bit too much fun one day teasing me by saying that a few of the allergies on the list might be psychosomatic.

His kidding didn't bother me, because I knew if I drank coffee, by the next morning I'd have pimples on my face. Psychosomatic or not, I wasn't interested in having a face full of pimples, so I just avoided coffee. Ironically, we discovered later that the culprit was actually the soy-based partially hydrogenated oil in the nondairy creamer. I knew if I wore perfume or was around someone with heavy perfume, I'd get a headache immediately or begin to sneeze nonstop, so I stayed away from fragrances. Keith calling these challenges psychosomatic, in private as well as in front of other people, didn't hurt my feelings until one particular exchange.

I had come home from a hike with a friend, and I noticed Keith had so kindly cleaned the house for guests we were expecting the following day. He'd decided to try something new on the carpet to make it smell fresh. He had purchased a carpet powder, one he thought smelled very mild, and had sprinkled it on the carpet in our downstairs bedroom and office. As soon as I walked into the house, the fragrance bothered me. I was only in the house for a moment, however, before leaving to have breakfast with the same friend.

When I returned from breakfast, the smell was more pronounced throughout the house. I opened all the doors to let air in, but that didn't diminish the fragrance. I opened both windows in our bedroom and office and hoped it would air out by bedtime. Unfortunately, it did not, so I asked Keith to help me blow up an air mattress we sometimes used for guests so I could sleep on the living room floor. Not only did he help get me set up in the living room for that night, but he decided to join me there as well.

The second night was similar for me but very different for Keith. Although he could no longer smell the fragrance in most of the house, as soon as I went into the bedroom, a headache ensued. I asked him to help me blow up the air mattress again so I could sleep in the living room once more. The first night he had helped me with pleasure and had even slept on the air mattress with me. But the second night he helped me begrudgingly, or at least it seemed that way to me, and decided not to sleep in the living room because it was uncomfortable for him. His response to my request let me know that although he made joking references to my "psychosomatic" reactions, he may not have been joking this time. Otherwise, I surmised, he would have felt bad that I continued to have to sleep on an air mattress and could barely breathe in our bedroom.

I waited for a good time to address the situation. I knew it was not ideal to deal with it that night because I was tired and hurt by his response. I went to him the next morning and calmly told him how his response had made me feel. I mentioned that the way he had handled my request for help the night before bothered me. It seemed as though he had concluded my issue with the fragrance was all in my head and he was frustrated by it.

"I'm not in the frame of mind to talk about that right now!" was his rapid response.

At that moment I could feel my hurt rising up and turning into anger, so I dropped the conversation. I wasn't dropping the issue permanently, but I just knew that moment wasn't the right time to talk about it. I continued getting dressed for work and presumed innocence. I trusted that this loving and kind husband of mine was not intentionally trying to hurt me and would be open and receptive to hearing my thoughts later, at which time I would address not only how I felt but what I needed him to do to make it right.

That evening after work, and before 10:00 p.m., I asked if he was ready to talk about it. He chuckled because he knew it was coming. He listened as I spoke from my heart. And he explained what was going on in his head, mainly work issues that were causing him not to respond to me in the kind and gentle manner to which I was accustomed. I told him it was clear to me that when he referred to some of my challenges as being psychosomatic, he was not always joking. At first he insisted he was, but then he realized, based on his response to me, that his initial statement may not have been true.

The end result: he apologized. I asked him not to use the term *psychosomatic* when referring to me or any of my idiosyncrasies, and he agreed. Done. End of discussion. Followed by a long hug, laughing, and tons of kisses.

You and your spouse have a lifetime together, and you will be confronted by many minor annoyances like this one. Are most issues really so pressing as to require a response at the exact moment? If an issue is actually that pressing, get it resolved in a peaceable manner at the time. If it's too late at night, save the topic for the next day. Unless an issue is life threatening, something you deem urgent, or a problem that prevents you from living peaceably (and honestly), just let it go. Presume innocence, remember timing is everything, and as the title of Richard Carlson's popular book reminds us, "Don't sweat the small stuff . . . and it's all small stuff."

──────── *Day Six Challenge Questions* ────────

1. "A molehill quickly becomes a mountain if we allow problems to continue mounting." Describe a time when you have experienced this truth in your marriage. What "molehill" (minor annoyance) quickly escalated into a "mountain" (major argument)? What was the result?

2. Consider the psychologist's two prescriptions for marriage: (1) resolve all issues and challenges by the end of the day, and (2) don't have any tough conversations when you're tired. What advantages would these two principles provide to your discussions with your spouse? How would implementing these strategies affect your conversations—and intimacy—with your spouse?

3. Discuss this chapter with your spouse and decide together that going forward you commit to resolve all issues and challenges when you are both in your best state of mind. Whatever cannot be resolved by the end of the day, either agree to disagree, forgive each other and let it go, or write up a new "work order" for the next day.

RULES OF ENGAGEMENT

by Keith Weaver

FAWN, MY WONDERFUL WIFE AND THE AUTHOR OF THIS BOOK, thought it would be beneficial for me to share my perspective as a man and husband in respect to how we intentionally created an argument-free marriage. Specifically, she asked me to share my thoughts about how we manage conflict. What I have set forth in this chapter are essentially our "rules of engagement," or our approach to resolving conflicts as they arise within our marriage.

Being sensitive to your spouse's perspective, honest about your own, and wise with your choice of words are characteristics that will allow you to ease into a calm discussion instead of crashing into a heated argument. No, I'm not in any way a perfect husband—at times I can be as thoughtless as the next guy. And not every discussion with my wife ends with complete mutual agreement. When Fawn and I have a discussion, however, I try to stay mindful of these principles as much as possible. And I have to tell you, in our marriage it works quite well.

A LITTLE HELP (OR NOT)
FROM CLIFF HUXTABLE

As I started typing this chapter, Fawn and I were vacationing in Charleston, South Carolina. It was really late and Fawn was asleep. I had my days and nights mixed up, as my mother would say, so it was the perfect time for me to work. Unfortunately, as I stared at the blank computer screen I couldn't think of what to write. I had the television on in the background when God unstuck my writer's block with—of all things—Cliff Huxtable.

I glanced up at a rerun of *The Cosby Show* and tuned in a bit. I had missed the beginning of the episode, but having seen most episodes of this show numerous times, I knew it was the one in which the family is preparing for the grandparents' fiftieth wedding anniversary.

In the scene I watched, Sondra and her then-boyfriend, Elvin, are fighting on the way to the Huxtable house, and the spat continues after their arrival. In a funny moment with Cliff Huxtable, Elvin says, "I'm confused about my role as a man." He explains that if he tries to take Sondra's luggage, she would say, "I've got this." But if he fails to open a door for her, she would be upset that he wasn't chivalrous.

Cliff advises Elvin that the woman is always right and, for the sake of keeping the peace, Elvin should just ignore whatever logic (or lack thereof) he may want to apply to any given situation regarding his relationship with Sondra.

The exchange between the two men is certainly very funny, and possibly even effective for those who are passive or disengaged. But outside of a sitcom, this is not an effective way to foster a progressive understanding (or oneness) with your spouse. Ignoring logic for the sake of avoiding arguments seems as if it would leave a person muted, confused, and perhaps even create a dynamic in which honesty is traded for peace.

If I were Elvin, I would choose to say something like this to Sondra: "Honey, can you help me with a challenge I'm having? I love you, and I really would like to exceed the expectations you have for me as the man in your life. For example, when I don't open the door for you, it's because I'm responding to the independence you seek when you tell me you want to carry your own luggage. But I realize that my choice not to open the door has upset you. I respect you, and my goal is to be a gentleman and your heart's desire. Could you please help me understand?"

Obviously this is much better than saying, "Honey, can you help me understand why you are completely nuts?"

In most cases the suggested approach would result in a calm-voiced conversation, and both partners would come to a better mutual understanding. Who knows? Making love might be an additional side benefit (not a bad trade-off, I'd say!).

Even if the reaction from your spouse isn't as positive as I think it would be, at least clear and honest discussion has prevailed, and this will benefit your relationship over time.

PRESUME INNOCENCE IN ALL SITUATIONS

My approach to Fawn isn't that different from what I suggested Elvin's response should have been. I presume innocence in all situations, meaning if our views are not aligned or her actions are not what I would have preferred, I presume there must be a really good reason behind it. Essentially, I give her the benefit of the doubt and approach all issues with a sincere interest in seeking a personal understanding rather than drawing a predetermined conclusion.

I assess the possibility (or even reality) that perhaps I'm seeing things incorrectly or there is no "right" answer—a glass half-empty and one half-full are still the same. I could still conclude in my estimation that I was right and she was wrong, but the benefit of presuming innocence in our conversation would be that my reaction to Fawn is more thoughtful and respectful, not simply a knee-jerk defense of my views.

This approach of presuming innocence in all our discussions allows Fawn and me to address situations with as much ease as possible, which more often than not results in clarity and agreement. And, unlike the Elvin and Sondra scenario, in which Sondra's inconsistent responses could have led Elvin to believe his love interest is inexplicable, spouses who operate from the presumption that each other's responses are perfectly logical heightens their understanding of each other.

While I tend to be an affable person, I won't go along just to get along. That simply isn't me, and I suspect that is true for most men. That being said, when I choose to communicate with Fawn using common courtesy, a desire to understand, and a softer approach in relating to my wife, it is an investment that always seems to be worthwhile.

Give it a try. If I'm wrong, it won't cost you anything. But if I'm right, it just might change everything.

—————— Day Seven Challenge Questions ——————

1. Have you, like Elvin in *The Cosby Show* episode, ever been completely baffled by how your spouse reacted to something? Describe the situation. What was the result?
2. Think of a time when you decided to ignore logic or sweep something under the rug for the sake of avoiding

an argument with your spouse. What effect did that have on your relationship with your spouse? How is the "peace" achieved by ignoring an issue different from the peace that comes by calmly talking through and resolving an issue?

3. Define the principle of "presuming innocence" in your own words. In what ways could you implement this principle in your marriage? What effects do you think the principle of presuming innocence would have in your future discussions with your spouse?

WEEK TWO

DREAM A NEW DREAM

DREAMS ARE INTERESTING. SOME OF THEM ARE OUR OWN, and many are those we've adopted as our own along the way. For the last twenty years, I've been an entrepreneur at times, and I've also run companies for others with an entrepreneurial approach. I began the Happy Wives Club blog in response to all the negative portrayals of marriage in the media. I never expected it to turn into such a popular blog. And even after it became successful, I refused to call myself a blogger. Refused.

At a blogging conference I attended a few years later, I was the only person in the room who wasn't a blogger. Well, technically I did the same thing as everyone else in that room, but I couldn't bring myself to claim that title. Maybe it's because so many view bloggers as people who sit around in their pajamas all day, eating bonbons and writing posts about their kids and cats. Yes, some do that, but very few do it successfully.

I realized that the reason identifying myself as a blogger was difficult for me was that I had always identified with the corporate world. My first company, opened when I was eighteen, had close to ten employees. From that moment on, my dream was to be successful in business. Here's the interesting thing, though: being a successful businessperson was never my initial dream. It was one I picked up along the way.

As a young girl, I loved to write. Every year for her birthday, my mom didn't want a gift, but she did want me to write her a poem. Poetry was how I expressed myself. Sadly, I stopped writing poetry when I began pursuing business. And now, two decades later, I don't even know how to begin to bring out the poet in me again. But I never stopped writing. It is in my heart. It is what comes most naturally to me. If I sit down with a piece of paper, no matter the time or the day, I will always have words to fill the page. I am a writer. When I published my first book, I became an author. And when I became a *USA Today* and *New York Times* best-selling author, I realized the dream that had long been buried inside was now ready to come out and play.

My life now looks nothing like I imagined four years ago when I was still a hotel general manager. I struggle daily not to start a new business but rather to focus on writing the best books and articles possible, because running companies is what I know. It is where my comfort zone is and what I did for so long. But with every passing day, I become more and more comfortable with dreaming a new dream. One that allows me to grow into the best writer I can be and to embrace the gift placed inside me at such an early age.

WHAT IS YOUR DREAM ABOUT
YOUR MARRIAGE?

What is the dream you dream about your marriage? Are you living it, or did you pick up another dream along the way? When you were first married, did you believe you and your spouse would look into each other's eyes forever and see a spark? Did you believe that you would hold hands wherever you went and sit closely next to each other every time you sat down? Did you think arguments would be few and far between? What is your dream marriage? Is it the marriage you are living?

Like a snowball going downhill, picking up additional snow along the way, sometimes what begins as our dream picks up so much more along the way, and before we know it, we're no longer dreaming our own dream. We look at other couples and compare their marriages to ours. In making that comparison, we diminish the value of our own marriage. And as we will see in day twenty-three, the more comparisons we make, the more our own relationship is weakened.

Over the years, I've learned the most about creating and maintaining genuine happiness in marriage by being around couples who have successfully done that for decades. And you know what they all have in common? They march to the beat of their own drums. They all dream their own dreams.

Even still, no matter how great a couple's marriage may seem, you should never compare your relationship to theirs. As in every other area of life, when you compare what you have to what someone else has, you always lose. If you have a great marriage and compare yours to those who seem less successful, you run the risk of setting up your relationship for a downfall. Have you ever noticed that so many people who esteem themselves or their stuff higher than others often lose what they cherish most?

On the flip side, if your marriage seems less fantastic than other marriages around you, *don't sweat it*. You have everything you need to create the marriage of your dreams, and you have the rest of your life to make it happen. It will happen, as long as you stay focused on your marriage and your marriage alone.

Keith and I learn from others. We even emulate things we've seen other couples do successfully. This is healthy and wise. But enriching our marriage with things we've learned from others is as far as we go. In every area of life, comparisons always prove to be far more costly than they're worth. After spending years interviewing couples in loving and happy marriages, I can say this without exception: couples who decided years ago to chart their own marital course have the happiest and longest-lasting marriages. These couples still believe in the dream they set out for their marriages many years ago.

What's your dream? What do you want out of your marriage? If you don't have it, why don't you?

Once you figure out what your dream marriage looks like, begin to think of what it would take for you and your spouse to work toward it. While you're thinking about that, may I suggest you add one thing to that dream, since you've made it this far into the book? Can you imagine how much better your relationship might be if you argued a little less and snuggled a little more?

BEWARE OF OBSTACLES THAT
CAN BLOCK YOUR DREAMS

Two of the main culprits that prevent us from dreaming the biggest dreams possible for our marriages are others' views on marriage and our tendency to compare our marriage to those of others who seem to have better ones.

When Keith and I were newlyweds, we were astonished by the number of negative comments we heard regarding marriage. When we were in our first years of marriage, we constantly heard snide remarks about how things go downhill from those early years. After we passed the newlywed years, we thought the comments would subside. But unfortunately they didn't. When we reached our tenth anniversary and were clearly still head over heels in love with each other, the comments stopped. I guess at that point people realized we weren't listening to their predictions of diminishing romance and passion in our marriage.

We live in a time when nearly half the people we encounter have already gone through, or are possibly on their way to, divorce. So they are simply speaking from experience. They don't mean to demean your love or your chance of remaining happily married until the end of your time here on earth. Most are simply speaking out of hurt. Knowing that allows you to love them in spite of their comments while not allowing their opinions to adversely affect your relationship.

There are only two people who can create the marriage of your dreams, and those two are you and your spouse.

Today is all about looking deep inside and sharing with your spouse what you believe your marriage can be—not what it should be, as that might come across as accusatory—and how you'd like to work toward creating this. Don't focus on the role your spouse needs to play in making that dream come true. You can only be responsible for your side of the marriage, and you need to trust that your spouse will do his or her part.

YOUR MARRIAGE IS UNIQUE

One of my favorite marriage writers, Maggie Reyes, says, "Marriages are like fingerprints. Each one is different and each one is beautiful. Your marriage is beautiful. Your marriage is wonderful. Your marriage is unique. So don't make your marriage look like a cookie-cutter image of any other couple's."

Recently, on the Happy Wives Club site, I published a popular article of Maggie's entitled "The Definition of a Happy Marriage."

> Let's start with a scandalous declaration shall we? The definition of a happy marriage is . . . there is none. There isn't one way to fold sheets, or climb mountains, or be a wife. There is only your way. And my way, and his way and her way. There is no wrong way either.
>
> What's absolutely perfect for me . . . has nothing to do with what is perfect for you.
>
> And that's okay.
>
> We cause ourselves so much pain by thinking and believing that we have to live up to our (divorced) Auntie's idea of marriage or my great grandmother's ideal relationship.
>
> We really don't.
>
> What we need to do is find what happiness and integrity means to us. And then do that.
>
> Define what love means to us. And then be that.

Maggie wrapped up her post with this:

> Marriage is a choice we make every day.
> Choose to make it your own.
> Whatever that means.
> And declare it wonderful.
> Or at the very least—custom-made. *Just for you*. Every day.
> Like a Love-Latte.
> The definition of a happy marriage is, there is none.[1]

I love her comparison of marriage to a "Love-Latte" because that's exactly what it is. You can create it just as your heart desires. If you throw out what others have told you about marriage—what it should and shouldn't be, what it can and cannot be—what are you and your spouse left with? If you throw out what others have told you should be your "roles" in marriage and go with what is in your hearts, what roles come naturally and feel right to you as husband and wife? What do *you* desire most for your marriage? And how can you, together, create the marriage of your dreams?

As William Arthur Ward famously said, "If you can imagine it, you can achieve it. If you can dream it, you can become it."

—————— *Day Eight Challenge Questions* ——————

1. What is your dream for your marriage? Take a few moments to reflect on this question and write down a few characteristics of your dream marriage. Now look at your list and compare it to your current situation. Is this the marriage you are living? If not, what aspects of your dream marriage are you not currently experiencing? Be specific.

2. Review the list you made in question one. Where did you come up with your ideas for your dream marriage? Are you trying to live out someone else's dream? Reflect on this statement: "Couples who decided years ago to chart their own marital course have the happiest and longest-lasting marriages. . . . They all dream their own dreams." How would the decision to toss the list you wrote and "dream your own dream" affect your perspective on your marriage?

3. Decide today that you will throw out others' expectations of what marriage should be and go with what feels right

to you. Discuss the following questions with your spouse: What do you each desire most for your marriage? How can you and your spouse, together, create the marriage of your dreams?

DEFINE YOUR OWN
FAMILY VALUES

"MY DREAM IS TO BE A STAY-AT-HOME MOM AND WIFE."
Those were the words I uttered to my loving husband more than ten years ago. His response? First laughter, and I mean the gut-wrenching, belly-laugh type. Then a look of utter confusion. He said, "Honey, I'm not trying to be funny, but you're not built to be a stay-at-home mom. Every day I'd come home from work and the kids would run up to me and say, 'Daddy, please save us from Mommy! She's trying to turn us into another one of her projects!'"

The pure horror expressed on his face while envisioning what our children would do instantly flipped on a light switch in my head. He was right. Oh so very right. I would probably drive our children insane as a stay-at-home mom. I know this, in part, because early into our marriage my one attempt at being a stay-at-home wife quickly went down in flames.

MY FAILED ATTEMPT AT STAY-AT-HOME WIFE

It happened in 2004, shortly after my abrupt resignation as the business manager of an award-winning restaurant. The restaurant was popular and incredibly busy, but I had no passion for it, and working around the clock in a business you have no passion for can wear a person down pretty quickly. At least that was my experience.

Following my decision to give back my minority ownership stake, Keith thought it would be a good idea if I took off a few months before returning to work. After all, I'd been working, sometimes two or three jobs at the same time, since I was a teenager. He had dreams of my resting throughout the day and being able to enjoy our time together once he got home.

That sabbatical was short-lived. Keith would probably tell you that it never happened. Every day when he'd arrive home from work, I'd be exhausted. I'd spend the entire day working on a new project, creating a plan for a new business, or in one case, hiring private investigators and consulting a defense attorney in an effort to free a death-row inmate in Texas. I'll admit, that last one was random. But that's what happens when you leave me at home and ask me to rest!

Within that first week of my so-called sabbatical, we both realized being a stay-at-home anything is simply not the way I'm wired. At least it wasn't then and it still isn't now, a decade later. Does that mean I won't be a hands-on mom if God ever allows us to have children? Of course not. Knowing me, I might even fall in love with attachment parenting in those first few years. If Mayim Bialik could do it while pursuing her PhD, surely I could, right? Who knows what will happen if we are ever blessed with children? What we do know is how I'm wired now, and clearly it would be in the best interest of our children, as well as our marriage, for me to continue to work outside of the home.

MY SISTER'S SUCCESS AT STAY-AT-HOME MOTHERHOOD

My sister, Christy Joy, on the other hand, is a wonderful stay-at-home mom of three. She's living the life of her dreams. Christy Joy being a stay-at-home mom was something her husband not only supported but encouraged. Yet at times she's been made to feel less than by women who'd determined being a stay-at-home mom was outdated. She was treated as if she'd single-handedly reversed all the strides we've made as women to be treated as equals.

But isn't that equality at its best? Having the ability to choose for yourself what *you* want out of life, marriage, and motherhood? After Christy Joy's third child, she began a thriving online fitness community, Pregnant Not Powerless. She wanted to contribute to the household income while not giving up on her dream of being a stay-at-home mom.

My sister and I are a lot alike in many areas, but in this area we're different. The fortunate thing for both of us is that we have always been strong in our convictions about what works in our households. We decided early on that we owed explanations to no one. God and family, then everything and everyone else. We remain confident we are doing what is right for our families.

EACH FAMILY HAS ITS OWN VALUES

Courtney Joseph, the founder of Women Living Well, loves being a homeschooling stay-at-home mom and wife with sole responsibility for domestic duties. It's been her desire since she was a little girl, and she's now living out that dream. The first time I met Courtney, I found it incredibly refreshing to see the pure joy in her eyes when she talked about being a stay-at-home mom and wife. When talk-show host Rachael Ray interviewed her and titled the segment "Time-Warp Wives," I thought, *What time warp?* This lifestyle still works beautifully for women who want and choose it.

The same excitement I feel when I finish writing a new book or when I team up with my husband to flesh out a business idea is what Courtney feels when she's cooking, cleaning, and serving her family full-time. Courtney loves her life and is the perfect wife for her husband. I love my life and am the perfect wife for my husband.

Another friend of mine, Doyin, who had taken on the role of stay-at-home dad, is a part of a new breed of dads (maybe not so new, but new to becoming a larger part of the population who are doing this) who have taken on an equal parenting role, from combing his daughters' hair and getting them dressed for school to making them dinner when they come home. I met him through a mutual friend not long after he launched his site, Daddy Doin' Work. It was fascinating to hear about someone who had taken on an equal parenting role while continuing to work full-time and was writing about parenting from a father's perspective. What was even more interesting was the day I met him.

I arrived at the Barnes & Noble at the Americana (local shopping center) in Glendale for a book signing. Keith and I were running a bit late. I'd blame our tardiness on the traffic, which was bumper-to-bumper, but it really was just poor time planning, because the traffic is always horrendous in Los Angeles. I walked through the crowd and hugged many people who had familiar faces. And then I saw someone I didn't immediately recognize. That was, until he began walking toward me with his six-month-old in a baby carrier tethered to his chest. One of his hands held the hand of his young toddler daughter while the other gripped a bottle he was feeding the little one in the carrier.

It looked like a scene out of an Adam Sandler movie. I looked at him, then down at his toddler daughter, then up at his daughter in the carrier, whose legs were bouncing up and down as he walked and whose mouth was dripping from having drunk too much milk, and I just laughed. "You're not kidding. You're really a daddy doin' work!" We laughed together, but truly, it was one of the most beautiful things I'd ever seen.

Before the birth of his first daughter, there is no one in the world who could have convinced Doyin he'd be such a hands-on (and quite frankly, such a dynamic) dad, but now he'd have it no other way. This is what works for his family. As more women climb the corporate ladder, there's no doubt we will begin seeing more equal parenting roles and more men staying at home as the primary caregiver of the children.

This reminds me of our friends Miriam and Efi. Not only do we love being around them (Miriam and I share a knack for calling things exactly as we see them), but they are brilliant about putting their family above all else, including tradition. Miriam and Efi set a family tradition as soon as their children were born. As is the case for most Jews born in Israel, most of Miriam's friends are meticulous about observing the Sabbath every Saturday and having dinner with family every Friday. But Miriam found it a bit difficult to always adhere to the exact days on their religious calendar. She and Efi changed the days to suit their family. They make sure the purpose and meaning of the various Jewish holidays are still celebrated, but they don't stress themselves out to make sure they celebrate on the exact day.

If a religious holiday falls on a Thursday but the entire family can't get together until Friday, then that holiday now falls on that Friday in the Gluzer household. Family and togetherness are the most important, and Miriam impressed upon me in our first interview that you can and should create your own family culture. You don't have to follow the crowd. It's certainly worked for Miriam and Efi and their children for almost four decades.

MORE THAN ENOUGH

Keith and I would love to have children. It is our hearts' desire to share the love we have for each other with a young one we bring into the world. But that hasn't been our reality. There is a yellow baby room that sits empty in a corner of our home. We began designing it while in the process of adopting a child being born to a mom with three children already; her youngest was just a few months old and she had no means to take care of them. We had decided to adopt after trying for some time to conceive on our own and had been successfully matched with a birth mother. After we met the birth mom and she decided we were the right parents for her unborn child, we began to prepare our home for our new bundle of joy.

Only that day never came. A few months before the mother was scheduled to give birth at a hospital right outside of San

Diego, Keith and I, along with his parents, drove to San Diego to join the mom at her upcoming ultrasound appointment. We checked into the hotel and waited for the details. We should have had them hours earlier and were beginning to wonder why we hadn't received a call. And then the call came. The mother had had a huge fight with the father of the child, the fight had turned violent, and the father had been arrested. Somewhere between the beginning of that fight and the end, the mother had decided to keep the child. Oh, how I pray for that child.

We turned to fertility treatments, and so far, nearly a dozen fertility treatments later, we've gotten oh so close but remain oh so far away. Thankfully, we decided early on that we would be perfectly happy with our family of two. We felt that our family of two would be more than enough for us. And although people often pity us for our inability to have children thus far, we determined long ago that our family values didn't require them. It would be amazing if we could have children, but if that's not in God's plan for our lives, that is most certainly his choice to make. And his decision to bless us with a happy family of two is more than we could have ever hoped or asked for.

Recently, after I spoke to a group of ladies and shared our fertility challenges, a woman timidly came up to me to express her gratitude for my sharing how Keith and I have come to embrace our family of two as beautiful, destined, and more than enough. Come to think of it, I don't think I've ever spoken on this topic in public without someone in the crowd coming up to me, usually with glistening eyes, to share her painful journey to motherhood. And my encouragement to her is always the same: "Your family of two is more than enough. Your life is already wonderful. You were blessed to find your soul mate and to marry your closest friend. A family of two is a blessing to society." And as if I could never say this enough, I usually repeat, "Your family of two is more than enough."

What do you and your husband do out of duty to others? What roles and patterns of behavior have you adopted within your family, marriage, or household because others believe they are the best ways? Once you begin peeling back the layers, don't be surprised if everything you've assumed to be right ends up being wrong for your family. Define your own family values.

──────── *Day Nine Challenge Questions* ────────

1. How are you wired—as a stay-at-home spouse, a working spouse, or a combination? Which option works best for your household, given your individual personalities and specific circumstances?

2. What aspects of your family life have you and your husband been doing out of duty to others? What values or roles have you adopted within your family, marriage, or household only because others believed them to be the best ways?

3. Set aside some time with your spouse to define your unique family values. What convictions do you and your spouse share about what works in your own household? In what ways do your family values differ from those of other families? Remember: once you and your spouse have defined and agreed on your own family values, you owe explanations to no one. You can be confident that you are doing what is right for your family.

TAKE THE ROAD
ALREADY TRAVELED

WHEN I BEGAN WRITING THIS CHAPTER, I WAS SITTING BY the Pacific Ocean among the stunning mountains and trees surrounding Montezuma, Costa Rica. Among the white-faced monkeys, geckos, exotic birds, and coconut palms sits a Spanish immersion school. I had spent many years desiring to be fluent in Spanish but making little effort toward that goal. But that month Keith's mom and I packed our bags, gave our hubbies a kiss, and headed out for one month to actively work on our fluency. In Los Angeles, it's helpful in business. If Keith and I are blessed with children, we hope to raise them bilingually, and because I only know "Spanglish," immersion was the best way to go for me.

A few days after arriving in Montezuma, an incident occurred that I thought about repeatedly as I began writing this chapter. Next to the school we were attending was a pathway through trees and a flowing river that led up a mountain to a cascading waterfall. A weekly trek to the waterfall followed by a swim in the natural pool below was a highlight for the students. Mom and I were both excited to go, so we got dressed and headed downstairs to meet the tour guides and other students at 8:00 a.m.

The day before our hike to the waterfall we passed by what looked like the entrance to the pathway, and Mom said, "That doesn't look like any place we should be walking." Indeed. But neither of us took the time to consider the sign written in Spanish (with an English caption beneath it), "*¡Peligro! Varias personas han muerto aquí. No escalar ni saltar.*" ("Danger! Several people have been killed here. Do not climb or jump.") Needless to say, the only way to get up was to climb. In spite of the sign, I was looking forward to the challenge and excited for the tour to begin.

Reading this, you might be thinking I'm the type of person who enjoys skydiving, bungee jumping, zip-lining, and all the other fascinating (yet dangerous) things some people enjoy. But I assure you, this waterfall hike was the most dangerous thing I've ever done intentionally. I may take risks in business, but not with my life. Shortly into our trek up the mountain, Mom slipped on a rock and her foot went into two feet of mud. When she pulled out her foot, her shoe, sock, and leg up to her knee were covered in mud. She continued on for a few more minutes, looked up at the rest of the path and the number of rocks we'd need to climb, and said, "I've had enough. I'm done. I'm going back."

Initially, her decision to turn around saddened me because I knew the waterfall, based on stories from other students, would be breathtaking. Within five minutes, however, I thanked God for her decision because the rocks became more slippery, the current of the water more forceful, and the climb a lot steeper. In many areas I had to grip the rocks below with both my hands and feet to keep from falling in the river or getting my foot caught between stones. Mom had definitely made the right choice for her. But I continued on.

There were twenty or so students making their way up the side of the mountain to the cascading waterfall and only two experienced guides. Sometimes I could see them and sometimes I could not. So I began to rely on something else: the path already traversed. Step by step, making the right decision on what stepping-stones to use and identifying what pathway was not safe became a lot easier, mainly because I was looking for the footprints of the many hikers who had gone before me.

If I looked closely enough, I could see the way in which most adventurists had chosen to climb, and I knew there was a reason for every frequented rock and stepping-stone. I began carefully looking for more footprints, areas that looked as though they'd been traversed time and time again, and those became my path. Arriving at the waterfall, I gazed at one of the most breathtaking panoramas I'd ever seen. And it was the first time I touched a waterfall.

My comrades had a blast. They all dove into the water, swam across to where the waterfall poured down, and jumped off rocks behind it in order to go through it. I took out my phone and began to videotape and document those moments. That was an experience I never wanted to forget. On the way back down the mountain, a thought shone in my head like a bright spotlight: *Take the road already traveled.*

As an independent person from the time I was young, much to my parents' and teachers' dismay, I've always prided myself in taking the road less traveled. Dreaming a new dream for my marriage and defining my own values for my family came easily to me. I'm a trailblazer by nature.

But what I realized at that moment was that there are times in life when taking the road already traveled, the pathway previously traversed, is the best way to get to your destination. And then I thought about this book. As I was making my way down the rocks and stepping-stones, making sure I had strong footing for each and every step, I wrote this chapter in my head.

LEARNING FROM OTHERS' EXPERIENCE

When Keith and I were first married, we began spending more time around couples who'd already been successful in marriage for at least a quarter of a century. We paid close attention to everything they had to say, as we wanted to be successful in our marriage and to enjoy every minute of it. We believed that if we could learn from the challenges and struggles others had overcome, we could avoid most of them and simply apply the principles these couples had discovered along the way. This is what we did, and more than a decade later it is what we continue to do.

We learned a few things immediately. One was that the couples who'd had five or more years to themselves without children seemed to fare much better in their relationships, indicating they'd had far fewer arguments and challenges along the way. We surmised this was probably because when two people are joined together, they bring in two separate "suitcases" (I prefer that word to "baggage") with their life histories: their relational histories, beliefs, and the way they like to do things. Those initial years are needed to merge two lives as seamlessly as possible.

Having children in the first few years seemed to challenge this process quite a bit. And although we also met many wonderful couples who'd had children in their first year, and even some who'd had children before they were wed, and we heeded their great wisdom as well, Keith and I decided we'd wait at least five years into our marriage before expanding our family. Who knew it would actually take eleven years and counting?

Another factor that stood out for us was that those who spoke about the possibility of divorce or maintained relationships with single people they could become, or had previously been, attracted to seemed to be challenged with thoughts of infidelity and in some cases acted on those thoughts. Consequently, we determined we would only have friends of the opposite sex whom we were friends with as a couple. Single male friends I had before Keith and I were married were left by the wayside and vice versa. And we never looked back.

One of the most important lessons we learned early on in our marriage was to surround ourselves with others who have marriages like the one we want to have. In an era when it seems that everything we read about and see on television regarding marriage involves arguments and infidelity, it was important to separate fact from fiction. We knew a lot of our friends were having challenges in their marriages, but we also knew there were some who'd figured out how to make marriage work and to love every minute of it. We sought out couples like this and continue to do so.

When I traveled around the world interviewing those amazing couples, I recorded their every word. I also made a mental note of the way they looked into each other's eyes, the respect they showed each other, and the way they gently caressed the hand, neck, and shoulders of their spouse.

SURROUND YOURSELF WITH HAPPY MARRIAGES

If you've made it to this chapter, I trust that during the past nine days in your marriage, you've learned a lot about your spouse and how you can work together to build a love that will last a lifetime. The next thing I encourage you to do is to search out couples who have the type of relationship you and your spouse want to have and then to spend time with them. You don't have to come with a list of questions; you don't want them to feel as though they're being interviewed. Just being around them will be enough. If you are watching and listening closely, you will find that those with happy marriages can't help but talk about their life together. And it's the little things they do, the way they seem to have their own language and movements that are in sync, that you want to take note of and see how you can replicate in your own relationship.

Marriage can be a lot of work. But it doesn't have to be. I am a firm believer of this. I was fortunate to grow up watching two parents who loved each other. I learned a lot from their relationship. You may not have had that benefit. But now is your chance to find others in your community, at church, or at your favorite local coffee shop. Begin to engage those happy in their marriage and surround yourself with more like them.

You know what they say: "Birds of a feather flock together." Join the flock of couples who are blissfully married, and put in the effort it takes to become one of those couples. Then when other couples begin looking for happy couples who live out the beauty in marriage, they will find you.

HEADING IN THE RIGHT DIRECTION

There is a time to be unique and to chart your own path. Every long-term successful marriage has this stage in common. And there is also a time to take the road already traveled. Although there were times when I couldn't see the guides on my waterfall adventure,

I never feared. Each time the bottom of my shoe landed in the middle of a footprint as I continued the hike, I knew that landing was safe. I knew it could bear my weight. And I knew it was headed in the right direction.

Although at times there is a fine line between emulating another couple and comparing your marriage to theirs, continue on. Remind yourself that you're not wanting to duplicate their marriage but to discover what has worked and how you can make similar things work in your own marriage. Each time I placed my foot atop one of the footprints heading up the side of that mountain, I was still charting my own path. My footprint was still unique and did not mirror the others exactly. And hours later, when other hikers began to ascend toward the waterfall, it would be my footprints they'd be following.

If there is only one thing you take away from this book, I hope it will be this: surround yourself with couples who have been happily married for at least a quarter of a century. Seek them out. Befriend them. And just enjoy time in their presence. They have a wealth of wisdom to share. And if your experience is anything like mine, every happily married couple you encounter will want your marriage to succeed—and not only to succeed but to be genuinely happy. And they will take you under their wings and help show you the way.

———— *Day Ten Challenge Questions* ————

1. "There are times in life when taking the road already traveled, the pathway previously traversed, is the best way to get to your destination." How does the principle of "taking the road already traveled" apply to marriage? What benefits to your marriage could you and your spouse experience

by following a path others have traveled rather than blazing your own trail?

2. Do you and your spouse currently spend time regularly with couples who have been successfully married for at least twenty-five years? If not, how could you begin to make this a priority? Ask around your community, church, or workplace to find a happily married couple who might be willing to share their years of experience with you.

3. When you find a longtime married couple who enjoy the type of relationship you and your spouse aspire to have, arrange to take them to dinner or spend time with them in a casual manner. Observe the little things they do to communicate love to each other. Learn from the challenges they have overcome together, and listen closely to the wisdom they share about how you can eliminate arguments and thrive in your marriage.

START A DAILY RITUAL

FOR MONTHS AFTER THE RELEASE OF *HAPPY WIVES CLUB*, I was asked by nearly every person I encountered who knew about the book, "So what's the secret to a happy marriage?" After I shared that, to my surprise, there were twelve common denominators among couples who had been happily married for more than twenty-five years, the follow-up question was about as predictable as the sun rising in Tucson: "What was your favorite secret you learned from the couples?"

That question always brought a smile to my face, as it caused me to look back over my journey and recall one of my favorite lessons. I'm not quite sure where I was when I had the realization. Maybe it was in the Philippines after interviewing a couple who'd just celebrated their fiftieth anniversary. Perhaps it was in Australia, following back-to-back interviews with happily married couples who have been in love longer than I've been alive. I'm not sure, but what I do know is that somewhere between Asia and the South Pacific, I had a huge *aha* moment.

I'd traveled all over the world to interview happily married couples before realizing they all shared one marriage secret I'd never heard about. Quite frankly, I don't even think most of them noticed that they did it. I wondered, *How is it possible that couples on six different continents are all doing this one thing, yet most couples married less than twenty years—including Keith and me—don't know about it?*

A MARRIAGE SECRET SHARED
AROUND THE WORLD

Before getting married, I heard about the importance of a weekly date night. I bet you've heard that many times too. And yes, that is hugely important whenever possible. Yet many of the happily married couples I interviewed didn't go on weekly dates. What each of them did instead, however, is an even better way to stay connected.

Every couple I've interviewed (happily married twenty-five-plus years)—from North America to South America, Africa to Europe, Asia to Australia—has a daily ritual. They make the time to do something together each and every day. Nothing fancy. Not necessarily getting dressed up or spending money at a restaurant. Nor spending hours in the kitchen trying to cook the perfect meal or dusting off the china. What these couples did was simple. It had been a part of their marriages for so long, some didn't even realize they had a daily ritual until I pointed it out. It was simply a part of the fiber of their marriage. Thinking back, I realized I'd actually heard about this marriage secret before I left Los Angeles on that journey. The first time I heard it was from a woman I met online.

Walking into a coffee shop just down the road from my

house, I started to feel excited about meeting my online friend. Though I hadn't yet personally met Miriam, I knew immediately we'd become friends. I couldn't possibly befriend each of the tens of thousands of women who were active members of the Happy Wives Club at that point, but something about Miriam drew me to her. She had a spark that came through in every e-mail. I don't mean she used a lot of exclamation points or all caps. There was just a vibrancy, an energy for life, that jumped off the screen.

The fact that we were meeting was happenstance. It turned out we lived close to each other, and it felt like a shockwave of delight would detonate if we got together. I wanted to light the fuse.

"How will I recognize you?" she had asked me.

"I'm easy to spot," I had replied. "Just look for the African American woman with green eyes. There aren't many of us around these parts."

She was there waiting for me, all fire and verve, a lovely light from Israel with three grown children and a husband who makes her laugh. The moment she spotted me, she began waving her arms in the air so frantically there was no way anyone in the coffee shop, including me, could have missed her. Standing no more than four feet eleven inches and wearing a loose black-and-green blouse that complemented her short black hair, Miriam lifted her arms wide for a hug. I quickly obliged. This was going to be fun. The excitement between us was like that of two old friends reuniting after thirty years.

We ordered, found a patio table in the California sun, and settled in while our hipster barista eyed us because of the emotional scene that had just erupted in front of his espresso machine. I sat attentively while Miriam started her story.

Born in Israel, Miriam learned early about the importance of having a strong family bond. Although she moved to the United States at a young age, she returned to Israel years later and met the love of her life, Efi. Their courtship began long distance and involved cassette tapes sent back and forth across the Atlantic. She told me about late evenings in her bedroom when she would pour out her heart, gather the noteworthy happenings, and capture her love on a thin strip of magnetic tape. She would imagine her love, across the ocean and over the desert, playing the tape over and over again.

She told me about the long wait for his replies and the elation of getting a parcel speckled in postage, ink stamps, foreign languages, and dirt smudges. As she played his messages back, a warm, gravelly voice would tell her of his longing, of his impatience and sadness from being apart. For a year, they longed to see each other face-to-face but had to settle for phone calls, letters, and cassette tapes.

Ten years after they wed in Israel, they moved to the United States. They brought luggage, their two bubbly children (the third would come a little later), a shoebox of cassettes, and Miriam's upbeat personality, her love of life, and what she calls good old-fashioned common sense. After hearing their unique story, I had many questions I wanted to ask her.

"What are the top five things in your marriage that have allowed you to stay happy for so many years?" Always the rebel, Miriam responded with six principles for a happy marriage: spend time together daily, give each other attention, have a hobby or social life outside of marriage, bond over common cultural similarities, have trust, and always show mutual respect.

It was that first one, spending time together daily, that caused me to pause. Of course, every couple spends time together daily. What was special about the time that Miriam was talking about—and that every couple I've interviewed around the world has told me about since?

Every evening Miriam and Efi eat appetizers together while sipping from small glasses of port. They tell each other about their days, sharing news about work, friends, and family. They let down their guards and talk about everything that matters to them. They cultivate a best-friend relationship. They go on dates. They meet each other for lunch when their schedules line up. In short, they are intentional with each other, and they don't let the host of outside forces erode the good thing they have going.

Although Miriam was the first person who told me about this ritual, she certainly wasn't the last. Around the globe I began hearing story after story of daily rituals from couples whose marriages were so magnificent I stood in awe. Each couple set aside a time daily simply to connect with each other. Nothing was off-limits. Partners shared each other's dreams and hopes. Discovering that so many successful marriages from earlier generations include this ritual made me wonder how our marriage would improve if Keith and I added a daily ritual.

THREE BENEFITS OF A DAILY RITUAL

What comes to mind when you think of the word *ritual*? Many people who hear the term are predisposed against it. When Keith and I were first married, every time I'd attempt to take something we enjoyed doing and turn it into a ritual (or *tradition*, as he called it), he'd protest because he feared that what we'd once enjoyed would begin to feel obligatory. Then I shared with him the three main benefits of establishing a daily ritual together, and he agreed this was something we should try.

1. *Daily rituals build trust.* When you get together with your spouse every day and talk about what has transpired during the past twenty-four hours and what's on the agenda for the following or current day, that communication provides transparency. It's hard to keep secrets when you are having meaningful and in-depth conversations every day.

2. *Daily rituals foster connectivity.* So many of us rush through life. We talk via text messages on our phones, e-mail, Twitter, Facebook, and other ways that don't involve face-to-face interaction. When you begin each morning with a cup of coffee or tea, even if you do nothing more than look into each other's eyes and take in the day together, you are building a connection. You are strengthening your bond.

3. *Daily rituals create longevity in relationships.* A *New York Times* op-ed recently sent to me entitled "New Love: A Short Shelf Life" reminded me why taking the time to stay connected throughout marriage is one of the greatest investments we can make. You don't have to wait until the kids are out of the house to rekindle your friendship. Stay connected throughout their childhood years, and your marriage and their lives will both reap grand dividends.

Immediately following my return to the States, Keith and I signed up for a fitness class and began taking it together at five thirty every morning. We decided that this class, followed by breakfast at home, would be our daily ritual. After a while, the 5:30 a.m. class became tough for me to attend because I often work so late at night. Now we take the class at different times during the day, but our Weaver Coffee Hour ritual, which is sometimes only thirty or forty minutes, remains the same.

Our friends Elicia and Dave put their children to bed each

night at eight o'clock on the dot. Then they melt into each other's arms on the couch and enjoy time with each other. It's the only time in the day they can claim all to themselves. We met a couple who go for a run every morning with their dog, Buster. We've watched them in the home stretch a few times and love that once they finish their last mile, they end their run with a high five. This time together allows them to chat about everything on their agenda for their day and anything else on their minds, other than catching their breath after a three-mile run.

After two years, I can tell you that having a daily ritual of spending time together changes everything—for the better. As the saying goes, "An apple a day keeps the doctor away." Well, when it comes to a daily ritual, it's like feeding your marriage an apple a day. Only this apple feeds your soul and keeps everything you don't want in your marriage far, far away.

There are 1,440 minutes in a day. If you can figure out a way to carve at least 30 minutes out of that grand total, it will do more for your marriage than almost anything else in this book.

Day Eleven Challenge Questions

1. Do you and your spouse currently have a daily ritual? If so, describe it on paper. If not, write out a few of the benefits you and your spouse could receive from implementing a daily ritual in your marriage. Be specific.

2. Discuss with your spouse the three benefits of the principle of a daily ritual, as explained in this chapter. If you haven't already implemented this principle in your marriage, ask your spouse if you could start a daily ritual. Brainstorm together: What kinds of things could you and your spouse

do together every day? Remember, your daily ritual doesn't have to be elaborate. It could be as simple as a morning cup of coffee or an evening walk.

3. What changes would you have to make to your current routine to make a ritual with your spouse a regular part of your day—such as waking up earlier, getting a babysitter, leaving work sooner? What preparations can you make in advance to ensure that these adjustments to your routine will not prevent you from your daily ritual?

Day Twelve

EMBRACE A DAY OF REST

IF YOU'VE EVER MET AN ORTHODOX JEW, YOU KNOW THAT observing the Sabbath day of rest is not optional for them. From sundown on Friday to sundown on Saturday, the world around them comes to a halt. It is forbidden to work. It is forbidden to switch electricity on and off. It is forbidden to travel in vehicles. It is forbidden to cook food.

I have always had a very deep respect for the Jewish practice of Shabbat, or Sabbath. Keith and I were humbled by this reverent tradition during a trip to Israel several years ago. For nearly two weeks, we traveled around the Holy Land from Tel Aviv to Jerusalem to Jericho and everywhere in between. The highlight of my time there, as an avid sports enthusiast, was hiking Masada.

After a physically exhausting but spiritually exhilarating tour of the mountaintop fortress of Masada, Keith and I returned to our hotel—only to be greeted by a dark lobby, lit mainly by candles. We'd been told by our tour guide that the entire city shuts down for Shabbat, but we didn't grasp the full extent of the shutdown until we were given the choice between riding on an elevator, which was preset to stop at every floor of the hotel since button pushing was not allowed, and taking the stairs. After observing the long line for the Shabbat elevator, we opted for the stairs.

WHY SHOULD WE KEEP THE SABBATH?

Unless you grew up in a religious household that strictly observed the Sabbath, chances are you've never experienced it. More important, it is likely you don't know the great benefits that observing this day, whether or not you're religious, can have for your marriage. When Keith and I began dating, he was aware that I observed the Sabbath, at least the Christian version of it, which was nowhere near as strict as the Sabbath practice of Orthodox Jews. I chose not to do any work one day a week out of a desire to honor this tradition first mentioned in the Ten Commandments. I decided that if God commanded a day of rest, then I would enjoy it with every fiber of my being. Plus, it gave me a reason not to wash clothes, clean dishes, or do anything else I didn't enjoy. It was the greatest excuse ever to spend an entire day doing absolutely nothing: God said it!

There are many schools of thought on whether a day of Sabbath rest is still a biblical mandate. DeVon Franklin, a dear friend of ours and an accomplished movie executive, is a devout Seventh-day Adventist, and if you sit with him for longer than five minutes, you will probably be convinced that all Bible believers should be observing this special day.

When DeVon is overseeing the release of a highly anticipated movie, as he has for blockbusters like *The Karate Kid* and *Heaven Is for Real*, he doesn't even look at the Friday box-office numbers until well into Saturday night. Can you imagine a studio executive turning off his phone and computer for a full twenty-four hours at the most important time of the week, when the weekend box office opens? Well, he does it every week and for his entire adult life has consistently observed what many still consider a commandment from God.

Seventh-day Adventist congregants, like DeVon, and Orthodox Jews, like those we had the pleasure of spending Shabbat with in Israel, adhere to the strictest form of the Sabbath rest. For those who aren't religious, or those like my father, who was a pastor but believed the Sabbath was no longer a biblical requirement, the point in observing a day of rest (or the point of this chapter, for that matter) may not be obvious, but stay with me here. I promise you will benefit from what you learn in this chapter.

TODAY'S STRESS EPIDEMIC

The Sabbath, a day of rest or a "stop day,"[1] as Dr. Matthew Sleeth, a former emergency room physician and author of the book *24/6: A Prescription for a Healthier, Happier Life* calls it, has more benefits for your marriage than you may realize. Initially, Keith didn't fully appreciate the importance of this day, but because of its importance to me, as a compromise he began observing it several years ago and will attest that he wishes he'd begun much earlier in his life.

For nearly two thousand years, Western culture stopped for a full day, most commonly Sunday, in honor of the Sabbath. Nearly every store was closed, few businesses remained open, and most workers ceased their work on this day. Then my generation came along and things began to change. We switched to working seven days a week, rarely taking time out to enjoy the fruits of our labor and to allow our minds and bodies to rest, and consequently stress and depression levels have reached an all-time high.

The cover story of *Time* magazine on June 6, 1983, called stress "The Epidemic of the Eighties."[2] And back then, we were just getting started. I was reading an article this morning by Dr. Andrew Weil confirming what I've heard many times in recent years, that stress has been linked to all the leading causes of death and that more than 90 percent of all visits to primary health care providers are due to stress-related problems.[3]

I've seen this play out around me firsthand over and over again. Just a couple of days ago I received a call from a family member who had been admitted to the emergency room for rapid heart palpitations. The distilled diagnosis: anxiety caused by stress. Think back to the last argument you had with your spouse. Think about your response only, not your spouse's. What were your stress levels? High or low? If your answer is low, you are most certainly in the minority.

The argument may not have even been about what was being discussed. A stress not even related to your relationship may have been the instigator. Keith learned early on in our marriage that a Fawn without rest isn't very pretty. Forget the outside, what comes out of my mouth is far less filtered. And believe me, I need a filter.

I need a day of rest like a swan needs water. It may not be required to live, but why wouldn't you want to take advantage of it? Years of experience have taught me I'm so much better with it. For the past seventeen years, I've made a day of rest a part of my regular routine. As a hotel executive, I found this proved difficult because there was an expectation that I would be available twenty-four hours a day, seven days a week. But I drew a line in the sand and made it clear my day of rest was nonnegotiable. After some time, I realized it would be nearly impossible to hold fast to this boundary I'd set for myself, so I left the hotel business. Maintaining a day of rest every week was that important.

I realized that without a day of rest, I'm just not as kind of a person. I'm less patient. My tolerance for folks who don't use common sense is, well, nil. As women, especially, we give and give and give. It's just how we're wired. If we do not take the time to refuel, to renew, to refill our coffers, we will run on empty. And a woman running on fumes is not a good sight to behold, for sure. Neither is a man at his wit's end. Once Keith recognized the many benefits of a day of rest for me as well as for him, he joined me in making this a part of our family tradition, and we've never looked back.

No matter how hectic times get for Keith and me, our day of rest is not negotiable. Unlike strict religious observers, we don't have a set time each week. Sometimes our day of rest might be from sundown on Friday to sundown on Saturday; sometimes it might be all day Saturday or all day Sunday. But what matters most is we observe it.

BENEFITS OF A SABBATH REST

If you and your spouse don't already take one day each week to slow down, turn off your phones, flip down the laptop, and just enjoy each other, allow me to encourage you to do so. This is one of the absolute best things you can do for your marriage and your pursuit of an argument-free marriage. Here are just a few of the benefits of observing a weekly day of rest:

1. *Your "available balance" will increase.* As in a bank account, if you are constantly withdrawing and giving to others, you will be left without anything for yourself. This day of rest gives you time to replenish your account so it is once again available for withdrawals without running the risk of overdraft fees.

2. *Your heart and mind will be refreshed by unplugging.* We experience information overload every day. We can barely calm our hearts and minds for an entire ten seconds. (Go ahead. Try it. I'll wait.) We are not machines; we weren't meant to process information nonstop all day. A day to yourselves, where you keep the world at bay, is one of the smartest things you can add to your schedule every week.

3. *Your level of patience and tolerance will increase.* Have you ever responded to someone in a way that later caused you to cringe? Chances are that you would not have responded that way if you had been well rested and full of life.

4. *Your energy will be renewed.* Rest for a day and you will undoubtedly feel the difference. You will have the energy to create the life—and marriage—you have dreamed of. It's as simple and as difficult as that.

5. *Your marriage will be strengthened.* Setting aside a day each week for "me" time, "us" time, and "anything that floats your boat" time will allow you to reconnect. And who among us couldn't use a little more one-on-one connecting time with our spouses?

6. *You will love better and with a fuller heart.* When you're exhausted, it's difficult to love your spouse with your whole heart. You just want to rest. This solves that problem and allows you to be the warm, loving, gracious person you were created to be.

7. *You will be happier.* Happiness is a natural by-product of gratitude. When you slow your world down for an entire day to live intentionally, gratitude will find its way in and that complaining

gene will find its way out. And the more gratitude you can sprinkle into your marital recipe, the better your results.

I challenge you and your spouse, just as I challenged Keith in this area years ago. Decide to give yourselves a *true* day of rest once a week. Don't do anything on that day you don't enjoy. Just take the day to exhale. Hold hands more. Pause and look into each other's eyes and be reminded of why you first fell in love. Commit to doing this for four straight weeks and see if you have any desire to go back to seven busy days a week. If you're anything like Keith, after a while you'll start trying to figure out how to squeeze in two Sabbath days a week.

———— *Day Twelve Challenge Questions* ————

1. Review the list of seven benefits to observing a Sabbath rest described in this chapter. Which one appeals to you most right now? Write it down. How could observing a day of rest with your spouse affect your communication with each other? What positive effects would a Sabbath rest have on your marriage—and on your personal life?

2. What obstacles are currently keeping you from observing a day of rest? How can you remove these obstacles or work around them?

3. Discuss with your spouse creative ways you can set aside one day a week together to rest from work and from the stress of daily life. Remember, it doesn't have to be Sunday; you can choose any day that is best for you. Then write your Sabbath day on your calendar and commit to it!

THE ONLY LIST
THAT MATTERS

THE LONDON PRESS WAS UP IN ARMS. I WAS GETTING CALLS and e-mails from radio stations, newspapers, television stations, and magazines from all over Europe and Australia. A well-known reporter with the *Times* of London did a feature story on me, the *Happy Wives Club* book, and the club itself. And although I spoke with the reporter at length on three separate occasions, when her story went to print, it was clear she had been looking for the most sensationalized version possible.

Here I was, a strong and independent woman, telling another strong and independent woman how important independence was even in an interdependent marriage. And what she took away from that conversation was the exact opposite. When the story went to press, she had a picture of me next to a picture of a woman decked out in a June Cleaver–type outfit, baking cupcakes.

As a person who can vividly remember the last time she baked (more than five years ago and for corporate clients of my hotel), I found a hilarious irony in that portrayal. Nonetheless, that's how I was portrayed, and what the *Times* of London writes is apparently considered fact the moment it goes to print. After that article was published, nearly every subsequent interview began the same way.

"Some say this woman is single-handedly destroying the feminist movement, returning women to the 1950s. She suggests every wife have a husband gratitude list." Well, at least they got one thing right. The husband gratitude list began as a blog post I originally planned to title "Top 10 Reasons I Love My Husband." Then, as I was writing it, I realized the list could literally go on forever, so I named it "Why I Love My Husband (the Possibly Never-Ending List)." I invited other bloggers to join me in creating their own lists on their own blogs:

Beginning today until I can't think of any more, I'm going to share at least one reason I love and adore my husband. *Why don't you join me?* What is it about your husband that makes you smile? What do you admire about him? What quirk or unique aspect of his personality would drive anyone else crazy but drives you nuts (in a good way)?

As I begin running my tally, I'd love for you to join me and keep your own "Why I Love My Husband" list. If you have your own blog, Facebook, Twitter, or Pinterest account, copy and paste the HWC button at the bottom of this blog post to let everyone know you're joining us in writing a list of everything that's supercalifragilisticexpialidocious about your husband. And for those who have never seen the movie *Mary Poppins* (how tragic), *supercalifragilisticexpialidocious* is just a bunch of root words thrown together: *super* (above), *cali* (beauty), *fragilistic* (delicate), *expiali* (to atone), and *docious* (educable). In other words, everything that makes your hubby rock!

And so my Husband Gratitude List began with a few simple statements:

1. He loves me exactly as I am . . . not for who I may one day become.
2. He's honest with me and honest with himself.
3. He has more integrity in his pinky finger than most people I meet each day.
4. He rides horses with me even though it's one of his least favorite things to do (because it's one of my absolute favorite things to do).

With every blog post, I continued the list. I did this for quite some time before realizing the entire Happy Wives Club community could benefit from keeping a similar list. What I quickly discovered through creating my own ongoing list was that what I had once viewed as ordinary became extraordinary when thought about intentionally throughout the day. The little things I might have taken for granted about Keith in the past—his taking out the trash, straightening up the house, taking my car in to be serviced—all became things that filled my heart with gratitude for my husband.

One of the greatest benefits of keeping a gratitude list is that it serves as a constant reminder of what makes your spouse so awesome. It's a constant reminder of why, out of all the people in the world, you chose your spouse. During those times when your imperfections glare brighter than your attributes, each of you can simply flip open your journal and look at your gratitude list to be reminded that *your marriage is bigger than that moment of discouragement.*

HOW TO MAKE A GRATITUDE LIST

A gratitude list is simple to compile. And *both spouses* should do it. All you have to do is begin. You can include something as overarching as the first item on my original list: "He loves me exactly as I am, not for who I may one day become."

You can also write down specific things your spouse did earlier in the day, like, "He spent hours organizing my desk, which I'd allowed to become overrun with notes and random pieces of paper." Although my list is quite long now, I thought I'd share a small section of it to encourage you to begin your own. Keeping a gratitude list does wonders for keeping your perspective right, especially during those times when your spouse falls short of perfection. After all, every one of us has flaws, right?

1. He is my biggest fan.
2. He never looks to point out what I've done wrong or the error of my ways. He looks for how he can build me up and make me feel great about what I do right.
3. He buys me bottles of every kind of water, except Aquafina and Dasani, the two he knows I don't like.
4. He texts me if a meeting is running later than he anticipated so I know to expect his call soon.
5. He is the most loyal person I've ever known.
6. When I travel on business, he always gives me 1,001 reasons to want to come home.
7. He's a strong man when it comes to the rest of the world but a complete softy when it comes to me.
8. When he picked me up at the airport this week, we walked out with me holding no bags and him holding

three. No matter how I tried to help, he simply wanted to take care of me.

9. He gets dressed for the gym early in the morning in the dark, so I can continue to get some rest.

10. He's patient with me and gives me the space I need to grow in my own time.

If you have a small notebook or your smartphone nearby, you can begin your gratitude list right now. And try to add to it as often as possible. I kept mine in the Notes section of my iPhone. As Keith did things throughout the day, I'd type them into my phone so I wouldn't forget. Sitting in the passenger seat of our car while Keith searched for parking near a popular hamburger joint, I pulled out my iPhone and typed how kind it was of him to take the time to drive to this place and deal with the parking, just because I said it might be nice to eat there.

Every little thing became a journal entry. The real fun comes in when you begin looking for things to add to your list. You will be amazed at how many considerate and helpful things your spouse does that you may have otherwise overlooked. And if your spouse is anything like mine, you'll soon realize there aren't enough thank-yous in a day.

In this world, we have an endless list of lists. To-do lists dominate most of our days. We also have grocery lists, school-work lists, and event lists. In this regard, I'm happy the media outlets in Europe were fascinated with my gratitude list, because it reminded me of its many benefits for every couple. Next time you think to argue with your spouse, attempt to do so while also being grateful for something he or she did earlier in the day. Sounds impossible to do, doesn't it? That's exactly the point.

Replace Complaining with Gratitude

My friends will tell you I'm the worst person to be around if you want to complain about your spouse. I'm from the school of thought that believes complaining about your spouse or marriage solves nothing and finding solutions to problems requires a steadiness, stability, and rationality, all of which tend to fly out the door the moment an argument begins.

Accordingly, I listen to my friends' complaints and then offer a different kind of response than they might be expecting: "Tell me something he does that's great. What was the last thing he did that you are grateful for?" When people begin looking for things to be grateful for, marriages are transformed.

A few months ago I received a message from a woman on my Happy Wives Club Facebook page who shared the story of how her marriage almost died and how she rescucitated it with more ease than she had thought possible. She and her husband were in their fifties, and her husband had been unemployed for almost two years. They had lost all their retirement savings. She said they went without food and electricity and sold their belongings just to survive.

She went on to share the residual anger she held inside that was taken out on her husband because he was the only other person in the house. She went to see a therapist, who suggested she write a long letter to him in order to get her anger out, but not send it. On the exact same day, she ran across my Facebook page. She realized it would take the same amount of effort to be angry with him as it would to learn to love him again. She "liked" the page and put the letter she had begun writing in the trash can. She decided to focus her energies on falling in love again.

She concluded her touching letter by saying she and her

husband were still in a bad place financially and, unfortunately, might still lose their home. But they no longer cared because as long as they were together, nothing else mattered. She closed her letter with, "Angels show up in the most interesting places."

Now, based on the unbelievable number of flaws my one little mind (and tongue) embodies, an angel is the last thing I would claim to be. But I am grateful I was there at the time when she most needed me, even though she only knew me as an obscure online profile. I was there to do for her what I do for my closest friends. I reminded her to focus on everything great about her husband.

What was—and is—so special about your partner that you forsook all others and pledged to be with him or her until death? When you are intentionally grateful for your spouse each day, your world and marriage can change for the better in an instant.

—————— *Day Thirteen Challenge Questions* ——————

1. What is so special about your spouse that you forsook all others and pledged to be with him or her until death? What is something your spouse does that is truly great? What was the last thing he or she did in your marriage that you are grateful for?
2. Now grab a small notebook or your smartphone and begin your own gratitude list. Write at the top: "Why I Love My Spouse (the possibly never-ending list)." Start your list with your answers to question one. Then continue to list at least ten things you love about your spouse. Review the suggestions in this chapter if you need ideas. As you begin looking for things to be grateful for, your marriage will be transformed.

3. After you've written at least ten things on your gratitude list, share your list with your spouse, perhaps during your daily ritual or day of rest. Regularly expressing your appreciation for each other in this way will help you on your journey to an argument-free marriage!

RELEASE YOUR EXPECTATIONS

OF PERFECTION

WHEN WE WALK DOWN THE AISLE AND PLEDGE TO REMAIN together "till death do us part," we not only walk away as Mr. and Mrs. So-and-So but also seem to return to our lives with a new moniker, "Mr. and Mrs. Fix It." Although most couples who marry love each other just the way they are, there seems to be an innate part of our personalities that somehow doesn't come out until we say those magical words "I do."

OPPOSITES DO ATTRACT

Not long ago, I was laughing about some of my quirkier personality traits and figured out which Hollywood characters they mirror most. Apparently I'm a cross between Lucy Ricardo, Joey Drayton (Katharine Houghton's character in *Guess Who's Coming to Dinner*), and Sheryl Yoast (the curly-headed blonde girl in *Remember the Titans*). Lucy is fun and witty, but is always getting into something. She concocts 101 ideas and gets excited about each and every one.

Joey's character in *Guess Who's Coming to Dinner* cares nothing about the outside world. She doesn't pay much attention to others' opinions and seems oblivious to reality. She is smart and not naïve in the least, yet she seems to live her life without reservation. She is fully aware of the thoughts and opinions of others, but chooses to care more about her own (and her fiancé's). Sheryl Yoast's character is only similar to me in her vocalness about her sports teams and her inability to bring herself to watch the most pivotal moments of a game. (I pause the DVR and wait to find out if my team won before pressing play.)

That's my personality, summed up by three distinctly different characters. Each of these characters would be considered unique and possibly fun. But combine all three and you've got quite the personality! The one similarity between all three characters is that they have very strong beliefs and are very secure in who they are. Not to mention that they're all incredibly talkative. My poor husband is dealing with a mix between Lucy, Joey, and Sheryl, with a double dose of opinionated.

Like Lucy, I am a bit of a klutz. I stumble over my own feet, run into walls, and often step on my husband's toes. For the first few years of our marriage, I accidentally kneed him in a very important place so many times that he'd brace himself whenever I came near. I pace in front of the television and yell at the players on my favorite team, the San Antonio Spurs, when they're giving up a game. I'd rather write a book than sweep the floor, and I'd rather grab takeout than cook and spend time washing dishes. I am not a fan of the word *no* or the phrase *you're wrong* and can list many instances in which I did not respond well to either. There are times when my thinking and my speaking seem to be one action.

What I just described about myself is the polar opposite of my husband's traits. He is calm, collected, rational, reasonable, and well-spoken, and he never, ever says anything without thinking about it first. He is a diplomat who weighs all sides of an issue before addressing it. He has great poise (he never runs into walls) and enjoys sports but is never fully invested in the outcome of the game.

He can sit in front of a television for hours, however, watching back-to-back episodes of *Landscapers' Challenge*. Really? Are you kidding me? Didn't he just see a garden that looked exactly like that in the last episode? He'd rather wax the car or pull weeds from the garden than sit and watch a movie (one of my favorite pastimes). But if you want to meet another person who doesn't like the phrase *you're wrong*, I'd like to introduce to you Mr. Weaver. This is a weakness we're both working on.

In an airport his semiclaustrophobic side kicks in, causing him to resemble a drill sergeant. He does not want to stop at any shops, get food, or even go to the bathroom. He wants to get to and from the terminal with as little distraction as possible. This is a challenge for me, because I like to look at everything, smile at everyone, and pick up candy and sweets in as many places as possible.

Initially it bothered me when he'd begin barking orders at me whenever we were in an airport. But then I realized how uncomfortable being around so many people made him feel, not to mention all the people bumping into his large, six-foot-four frame as we walked. Now I make a conscious effort to walk quickly with him to the gate before commencing my search for the best candy, sweet, or treat.

CELEBRATING OUR DIFFERENCES

When Keith and I were first married, we couldn't have been more different from each other. But over the years we have begun morphing into each other's likeness. The transformation is amazing to watch. We still have a lot of differences, but we have found ourselves sharing more similarities with each passing day. That has been a natural progression, because we've chosen to accept each other's differences. His uniquenesses don't annoy me because I understand they are a part of who he is, and vice versa.

A friend of mine said to me years ago, "If the two of us are identical, then one of us is unnecessary." Sometimes we need a reminder that the qualities that make our spouses different are also what make them great. Do we think so highly of ourselves that we want our spouses to be just like us?

Dr. Gary Chapman says in his book *The Family You've Always Wanted*, "An essential ingredient of intimacy is allowing your spouse to be himself without striving to conform him to your ideals. In intimacy, we try to grow closer together, not to eliminate the 'otherness,' but to enjoy it. Men and women are different and we must not, even with good intentions, seek to destroy those differences."[1]

In spite of my many known flaws, I believe the reason the phrase *you're wrong*, or anything similar, bothered me so much is that it stood contrary to my desire for perfection. For years, I denied being type A. Then I took a personality test administered by my former hotel company and discovered that not only was "driver" my number one personality trait, but it had such a high percentage in my profile that my "amiable" personality trait was almost nonexistent.

In order to release my expectations of perfection in Keith, I had to first learn to do that with myself. Releasing the expectation of perfection in ourselves and in others may be one of the most difficult tasks for women to master. At least that is the case with all my closest girlfriends. I'm not sure how or why so many of us grew up desiring perfection, especially in what we all know to be an imperfect world. In theory, we accept that we're imperfect people. And yet we still try to reach perfection in nearly everything we do, and we tend to have the same expectations of others. It is generally our expectations of perfection in others that fail us, not the actual people.

I am a recovering perfectionist. I phrase it this way because perfectionism is like an addiction, and it can be incredibly difficult to kick the habit. When Keith and I were first married, I didn't realize this about myself. Whenever Keith would point out an area he thought I could improve, I would immediately turn the tables around and point out a similar area in which he could use a little work.

The desire to be perfect was one of my greatest flaws in the early years of our relationship. So much so that it made me defensive and made Keith reluctant to share his less-than-positive thoughts with me. That was, until I had an aha moment. I realized I could never change or improve another person—that must be his or her own work. I could only change and improve myself. I didn't need to point out Keith's imperfections as a defense mechanism to keep him from pointing out mine. Being imperfect, I discovered, was A-OK. It was a reminder that I was only human.

ACCEPT CONSTRUCTIVE CRITICISM FROM YOUR SPOUSE

Welcoming constructive criticism from my husband—whom I know loves and adores me to pieces—rather than resisting it has made me a better person. Reminding myself daily that I am a work in progress and will never be perfect, nor should I ever strive to be, has allowed me to fully enjoy life without this unrealistic burden.

These days I wait for Keith to inquire about an area in which he might have room to grow, and then I gently offer him my input, letting him know I still love him exactly where he is. I give him plenty of room to make any changes in his own time, at his own pace. And he, in turn, does the same for me, which frees me to just be me—one million flaws and all. I can spend my time basking in everything delightful about him and know that his flaws will decrease as time goes on, just as mine will.

There is something oddly freeing about focusing on what is great about those around you while simultaneously accepting constructive criticism about yourself from people who love you. This attitude is rewarding not because you want your closest friends and family to point out every area in your life that could use some growth, but rather because inviting this type of feedback allows you to hear what others are probably thinking but may not be candid enough to say.

Accepting yourself as a work in progress takes the pressure off you to be perfect, which in turn removes your expectation that others, especially your spouse, will also be without flaws. And when you let go of your hope for others to be perfect, they naturally bestow a similar grace upon you. Release your expectation of perfection in yourself and your spouse today, and watch the dial on your happiness meter increase.

Where Keith is weak, I am strong, and where I am weak, Keith is strong. Our differences balance each other out this way. Together we are wiser, richer, and stronger than if we were by ourselves. That is one of the beauties of marriage. The power of two is greater than the strength of one.

A NEW PERSPECTIVE ON YOUR DIFFERENCES

The next time your spouse does something differently than the way you would do it, rather than stewing, try considering how the action makes your spouse special. Marvel in the unique characteristics of your spouse and accept them. Don't try to change them or require perfection. Your spouse will grow over time. Just be patient. Today I run into fewer walls, step on Keith's toes with less frequency, can stomach the word *no* and the phrase *you're wrong*, and only yell at the Spurs when they are in the NBA Playoffs or Finals and they are giving up the game!

It's not perfect, but for me it's growth. For Keith, it shows I want to be better, I desire to please him more, and I will diligently work at succeeding in both.

———— *Day Fourteen Challenge Questions* ————

1. In what ways is your personality different from your spouse's? To make this conversation a little more fun, discuss with your spouse which TV or movie characters you are most like and which ones your spouse is most like. How do your differences complement each other? How do they cause frustration in your relationship?
2. Are you sometimes a Mr. or Mrs. Fix It, attempting to "fix" the flaws you perceive in your spouse? Do you become frustrated when your spouse doesn't measure up to your expectations? Describe a time when an unmet expectation led to an argument with your spouse. What could you have done differently in that situation? If you applied today's principle of releasing your expectations of perfection, how would that affect your future conversations with your spouse?

3. "Reminding myself daily that I'm a work in progress and will never be perfect, nor should I ever strive to be, has allowed me to fully enjoy life without this unrealistic burden." How could you, too, remind yourself daily that you are a work in progress? Consider writing "I'm a work in progress" on a sticky note and putting it somewhere you will see it every day.

WEEK THREE

SPEAK THROUGH A FILTER

NOT LONG AGO KEITH HOSTED AN EVENT FOR HIS COLLEAGUES and local elected officials. The event had begun a half hour or so before I arrived, so Keith was busy walking throughout the reception area, greeting all the guests. His employer definitely got two for the price of one when we got married, because the moment I arrived I began doing the same. Keith can only make it around to so many people, so as usual, we divided and conquered.

As we were walking through the crowd, one of Keith's colleagues stopped us. She was holding a folded newspaper and started sharing why she had brought that newspaper with her. "Picture this," she began. "I was going through the Johannesburg airport on my way back from Cape Town, South Africa, when I saw someone on the cover I thought I recognized."

She continued, "I picked up the paper and looked at the name mentioned on the cover story and realized, *That's Keith's wife!*" She then flipped open the newspaper, and there it was, on the first page, a huge picture of me side by side with a housewife circa

1950. Above my picture, in huge letters, was the headline "Love More, Complain Less, Suppress Everything."

The article was similar to the original one in the *Times of London*, but at least it got part of the story right. "Love more": yes. "Complain less": oh, goodness, yes. "Suppress everything": not a chance.

KEEP YOUR "RUG" CLEAN

Keith and I have to have one of the cleanest rugs because we keep the surface clean and refuse to sweep anything under it. From our very first telephone conversation, which happened before we met in person because we were set up, Keith knew I wasn't like any other woman he'd ever met.

Keith, a man who hates talking on the phone, stayed on the line with me for three hours straight. He was fascinated, to say the least. Maybe it was my proclamation that I wouldn't sleep with him before marriage. That'll get anyone's attention on a first call. It also could have been how frank I was about my lack of desire to waste time going out with anyone I couldn't see myself marrying, and my view that I was perfectly content spending time alone and could pay for my own meals so I had no problem enjoying dinner for one.

Before we even got thirty minutes into our first call, we knew we had a connection. So imagine his thoughts when at the end of our most perfect call, three hours later, I concluded with, "If you wake up tomorrow and have this weird feeling that you shouldn't call me again, go with that. I won't take it personally. I prayed long ago that God would simply close the door on any man who wasn't my future husband so I wouldn't waste time. And God has answered that prayer for the past five years."

It took him three days to call again, but once he did, we both knew this wouldn't be a fling. Can you imagine if that woman he met over the phone—the one who intrigued him more than any woman he'd ever spoken to—all of a sudden began sweeping things under the rug once we said "I do"? Sweeping things under the rug only hides the dirt.

"Suppress everything": no, thank you.

Speak Through a Filter

In addition to "love more" and "complain less," here's one more piece of advice I'll add to the list.

Learn to speak through a filter: absolutely.

As you can probably tell, when Keith and I first met, I had no filter. I'm not kidding. No filter at all. I'd always reasoned that being an honest, open person was much better than sugarcoating my words. I'm still not very good with sugarcoating or tying up my words with a bow, but I have learned the importance of speaking through a filter. Of the many qualities I've picked up from my husband, this has to be the best one.

Keith and I have a tradition we've honored since our first year together. Every year on December 31, before attending a friend's annual New Year's event, we go to a casual restaurant to review our goals for the previous year and to establish new ones for the upcoming year. We pull out an index card. On one side of the card, we write all our individual goals. *Become fluent in Spanish* and *Get into the best shape of my life* were two of the five on my most recent list. On the flip side, we write a list of things we'd like the other person to work on in the coming year.

The first year we did this, it was a hard pill to swallow. Even though the list was fully contained on only one side of a three-by-five-inch index card, Keith's list of improvements for me seemed so long. And at the top of that list was learning to think before I speak. What a novel thought. My only saving grace, in our first ten years of marriage, is that although I always said what was on my mind—and still do—I said it with the greatest amount of respect.

TREAT YOUR SPOUSE WITH HONOR AND RESPECT

Not long after I began the Happy Wives Club, a photographer from a local paper came to our home to take pictures for an article. During our time together, he shared that he and his wife had just been in an argument over dinner the night before. She'd taken the time to cook a gourmet meal. When she was ready to serve it, he continued working because he wasn't ready to eat. She became frustrated. He responded in a like manner, and as is usually the case in these scenarios, an argument ensued.

Repeating words I'd once heard a counselor speak to a feuding couple, I posed one simple question to this newly married photographer: "Think of someone you hold in high esteem. The president. The chancellor of your university. Your pastor. Your rabbi. How would you have responded if this person, for whom you have enormous respect, called for you and said, 'The meal I was preparing for dinner is now ready'?" The photographer thought about it for a brief moment, gave an understanding smile, and then conceded that he would have gone to the dinner table immediately.

I reminded him that his wife was the only person he chose and subsequently pledged to be with for the remainder of his life. He wasn't given an option in choosing his parents or siblings. He didn't have the deciding vote in who would be his country's president. He likely had no say in selecting his university's chancellor. But he held each of them in higher regard than he held his wife, the one person he had the pleasure of choosing and who had also honored him by reciprocating in that choice.

"We tend to take our spouses for granted," I told him, "because we assume they will always be there. And we hope they will. But if there is anyone we should hold in high esteem, it is the person who pledged to be with us in good times and in bad, in sickness and in health, until death do us part."

These were not just the words I said to the photographer. They are words I continue to live by each and every day. Keith and I both speak to—and treat—each other with the greatest amount of respect.

There is no one alive I respect more than my husband. In my eyes, he is one of the most brilliant men to have ever walked the face of this earth. He's kind, compassionate, graceful under pressure, and untarnished under fire, and he can change the world with just one smile. My respect for him could be no greater than it is. Wherever he goes, I will go. Whatever he chooses to do, I will assist him. If he makes a mistake, we clean it up together. I am his partner in every aspect of life. I respect him to the utmost. Although I didn't have a filter and said what was on my mind, it was always from a place of honor and respect.

NO JUDGMENT. LOVE. GRACE.

My challenge—and the reason Keith continued to put "learn to think before you speak" on my index card nearly every year—is that although my respect for Keith naturally caused me to speak through a filter with him, when I spoke to everyone else it was like the Wild West. If I was talking, you might want to duck so as to avoid getting struck by my tongue! Finally, I realized that thinking before speaking is a skill that every wise person who has ever lived has mastered.

A couple of years ago I wrote on my index card, which contained all my goals, an acronym that has begun to govern every aspect of my life: NJLG. This acronym has changed the way I speak to people and often stops me cold in my tracks.

NJLG: No Judgment. Love. Grace.

Every word. Every thought. I now run them through my NJLG filter. I ask myself, *Am I judging? Are the words being spoken in love? Is every word seasoned with grace?* Grace is powerful and, when administered generously, possibly one of the greatest gifts in marriage. If Keith had not extended grace to me so often during our first ten years of marriage, I have no doubt I would not have been able to write this book. The authenticity of the words in this book are a result of my striving to be the best wife I can be and depending on the grace of my husband when I fall short.

I will be the first to say I fall flat on my face with this at times. I fail in a major way. I forget to pause and ask myself those three important questions before I part my lips. But then I quickly regroup and do my best to begin anew. And when I fail with Keith in this way, I am so thankful that he immediately employs a similar filter strategy for his response.

Like a water filter, your words filter needs to be replaced regularly to continue purifying. I must continuously remind myself to use this filter, and when I forget, I must immediately place that filter back on my lips to ensure no additional words leave my mouth without first running through it. It's not always easy, but as I've matured in life, I've learned it is absolutely necessary.

If there is one relationship in your life that deserves an NJLG filter, it's the one with your spouse. Do not judge. As Keith shared in his chapter, presume innocence. Speak in love. Administer grace with your words. If you can manage to remind yourself daily to place this filter over your lips, it will be hard for you to unleash a flurry of words you'll later regret.

———— *Day Fifteen Challenge Questions* ————

1. Do you carefully weigh your words before speaking, or do you usually speak your mind, no matter the cirumstance? Be honest with yourself as you consider the answer to that question. What is the difference between being an honest person and being too candid?

2. What are some of the advantages of "speaking through a filter"? In what ways would your conversations with your spouse be different if you chose to speak through a filter rather than blurt out whatever is on your mind at that moment?

3. In your conversations with your spouse, begin to run your words through the NJLG filter (No Judgment. Love. Grace.) described in today's reading. Before you speak to your spouse, ask yourself, *Am I judging? Are my words being*

spoken in love? Is every word seasoned with grace? If your thoughts don't pass the NJLG test, then don't say them. After a few weeks of using the NJLG filter, you'll experience more love and fewer arguments in your marriage.

GET A CLUE (THEN A CUE)

TODAY'S REALITY SHOWS FOCUSED ON MARRIAGE ARE ENOUGH to make me cringe. It's like watching a train wreck. You can't help but get pulled into the drama, but then you quickly realize that nothing good can come from this. Fighting, infidelity, and disrespect, along with all the other negative behaviors I hope aren't in your marriage, are on full display in the most exaggerated way. Of course, reality television writers come up with scenarios to create drama. They edit down hundreds of hours of footage to the few hours that will be aired throughout the season, and what we see are the worst, the most dramatic.

Reality television shows like *The Real Housewives* franchise are an incubator of drama, which would explain why more than 50 percent of its stars are divorced within a couple of years of being on the show.[1] I remember watching those shows and wondering, *How can any couple argue this much and remain together?*

Have you ever wondered why some couples argue nonstop and others argue very rarely? Over the years this question has caused me to pay a great deal of attention to couples on both ends of the spectrum. And I have discovered there is a commonality among those who have mastered the art of easing into a discussion rather than crashing into an argument. The first thing I noticed is that they shift the focus from their spouse to what they could have possibly done differently. They try to see the situation from their spouse's vantage point.

Although we've not had many major conflicts in our marriage, God forced me to see things from a different perspective, permanently changing my responses to Keith.

SHIFT YOUR FOCUS

We were living in a small home in Sherman Oaks, California, an area in northern Los Angeles County, and slowly over time, Keith's snoring began to get louder and louder. I rarely, if ever, slept through the night and was tired all the time. We'd tried everything we knew to help him stop snoring. My patience began to wear thin as the number of sleepless nights began to mount. One night I tossed and turned, placing pillows over my head, squeezing his nose to force him to breathe out of his mouth. Anything I could think to do. All I wanted was some sleep!

He, on the other hand, slept contentedly, oblivious to his overwhelmingly loud inhales and exhales. One morning, after yet another sleepless night, I turned to him and I can't remember exactly what I said under my breath, but I assure you, it wasn't pleasant. I remember him saying, "What's wrong with you?" I jumped out of bed and exclaimed, "I'm a woman deprived of sleep!" With that, I hurried to the bathroom before the law of acceleration could kick into full gear.

As I began preparing for work, I could hear a soft voice: *Fawn, you know you shouldn't have spoken to Keith like that.* But rather than heed that voice immediately, I lost it, seriously. But not with Keith. I lost it with God. Note to self: never yell at God; it's not helpful. "Well, God, you also could have allowed me to sleep, but you didn't! I've been praying over and over that you would make him stop snoring. Every day I pray the same prayer. But do you make him stop snoring? No! You just allow me to suffer." Can you imagine talking to God like that? Yes, not one of my better moments.

This internal yelling session went on for a moment before I calmed down long enough to hear, *Why don't you stop focusing on what's wrong with him and focus on yourself?* Now that was an interesting suggestion, I thought, given I wasn't the one snoring. Nonetheless, that evening, instead of praying that Keith would stop snoring, I asked instead that God would keep me from hearing Keith's snoring. What I wanted to achieve as the end result of my prayer was the exact same as before. I wanted to get some rest. But this time, instead of focusing my prayer on changing Keith, I focused it on changing me.

I'm sure you know what happened that night: I slept like a baby. This continued for quite a while before I began hearing the snoring again. I'm not too sure what happened or what lesson was to be learned from my starting to hear his snoring again, but I discovered an amazing invention. Earplugs! Mack's Pillow Soft silicone earplugs, to be exact. They work every night and I'm fully rested in the morning. Sometimes your spouse's "problems" can be easily solved by shifting the focus.

PAY CLOSE ATTENTION TO YOUR
SPOUSE'S MOOD CHANGES

Then there are times when focusing on your spouse is exactly what is needed. That is the second thing I noticed about couples who do not argue. They pay close attention to their spouses and any mood changes they might be having. They ask themselves, *Could this negative change in my spouse's attitude or mood be something caused by me?* And if they can't pinpoint something they may have done to frustrate or disappoint their spouse, they will simply ask their spouse this question and then listen.

This is exactly what happened to me not long ago. I noticed Keith responded to something positive I shared with him in a less-than-enthusiastic manner. The first thing I did was ask myself the above question. I couldn't quite put my finger on his lackluster response, so I simply posed the question to him. As it turned out, a response I'd given him in a discussion earlier that morning had disappointed him. And because I asked the question, we were able to comfortably segue back to that conversation and this time end with a resolution that worked much better for him.

Our friends Kim and James do this beautifully. They are so in tune with each other that if either is having a bad day, the spouse's first instinct is to figure out what is wrong with the other person, not to accuse the spouse or take the spouse's response personally. Whenever Keith and I get together with them, it's very relaxing because there is such great freedom in their relationship. There's no tenseness left over something that occurred earlier, something that has been left unsaid or unresolved. I've always found it incredibly difficult to sit with couples who are trying to pretend that everything is wonderful when there are clearly problems beneath the surface.

Get a Cue

A third thing I've noticed about couples who have conflict resolution down pat is that many of them have worked out a cue.
When out in public, they have a private cue between each other
that lets the other person know if he or she has unintentionally
said something that may have bothered the partner or hurt his or
her feelings.

That cue has saved me on many occasions. Although I do my
best to consistently speak through a filter, every now and then my
filter falls off and what comes out of my mouth is less than ideal.
There are other times when someone rubs me the wrong way,
and instead of responding with grace, I begin to get tense and my
body language shifts. Keith can see the shift while it is happening
and will gently give my leg two quick squeezes. The moment he
does that, it's like being awakened from a trance.

I use the exact same cue with Keith when he's making jokes
he thinks are funny that may not be funny to me. By giving his
leg two quick squeezes, or giving his hand two quick squeezes if
we're standing, I let him know that I'm not quite as amused as the
other listeners to the story may be.

In private we have another cue. We call each other by our first
names. "Fawn" is all Keith needs to say to get my attention. When
I've done, or am doing, something he's not very happy about, I
know it the moment he calls my name. As soon as I hear "Fawn"—
instead of "honey," "baby," "my love," or any of the other pet names
he calls me—I know it's time for me to *get a clue*.

There are many cues you can adopt. The very first time I
saw this in action and recognized what was happening was with
a well-known singing duo who had been married for forty years.
We were attending an event, and as the husband, who was being

honored, stood onstage thanking people, I glanced at his wife, who was giving him a cue that was clearly between just the two of them. She rubbed the right side of her nose with her thumb two times and then pointed to someone sitting in the crowd whom he had missed. He immediately thanked that person. Then moments later I saw her do that nose thing again and point to another person. That was their cue. Though it might seem unusual, any cue that works for a couple who have been married for four decades must be a pretty good one.

BE PATIENT WITH YOUR SPOUSE

The fourth thing I've noticed about couples who argue the least is that they extend a great deal of patience to each other. Margaret Thatcher once said, "I am extraordinarily patient, provided I get my own way in the end." Now, that may have worked for Margaret Thatcher, but in a marriage we will not always get our own way. However, it's not about each spouse getting his or her individual way. It's about discovering "our way" in everything, and that takes not only patience from you and your spouse but patience with yourselves and growth within your marriage.

The greatest joys and benefits of life require patience. Farmers are a great example of people who must master the art of patience. Personally, I don't know how they do it. But they know there is a specific time to plant the seeds, a time to water, a time to plow, and a time for harvest.

Farmers appreciate every season for what it contributes to the ultimate goal: a fruitful harvest. Many farmers work all winter and spring waiting for the summer's manifestation of their labor. They work feverishly day in and day out for two seasons without seeing results, but they are patient because they know that what they are sowing will eventually produce a good crop.

Two things in life will always require patience on our part: marriage and children. Most husbands and wives were raised differently, think differently, and communicate and act differently. These differences are what make marriage so great.

Every spouse requires patience. The day I took to the hills of Thousand Oaks to walk my hurt away, I knew if I came back too soon I would say something to Keith that I would later regret. I knew my words would hurt him. I relied on my patience to thwart a potential argument. Keith extends the same gift to me. I will be the first to admit I have a lot of quirky ways. Some of these traits would frustrate Keith tremendously if he did not exercise patience in our relationship.

If we want to have and maintain harmonious relationships in the workplace, among our friends, and with family and others around us, we must learn to be patient. Our spouses put up with our idiosyncratic ways, our not-so-great-smelling breath in the morning, and every not-so-cute thing about us. They deserve our patience. If we are patient with anyone, it should be with the person who lies beside us in the middle of the night and, rather than yelling at us for taking the covers, gently pulls them back. It is time to freely give to our spouses what they deserve, if for no other reason than they've dedicated their lives to a relationship with us.

Knowing what annoys your spouse and doing your best not to do that is getting a clue. Finding a common signal you can both use when out in public and you do something that bothers your spouse, and vice versa, is getting a cue. And what allows you to be successful in doing both is the same thing that is required when pursuing success in business, raising kids, or any other area of life: patience.

——— *Day Sixteen Challenge Questions* ———

1. "Sometimes your spouse's 'problems' can easily be solved by shifting the focus." Describe a time when, like the snoring incident, you became angry with your spouse over something he or she did or still does. Now turn the situation around and consider it from your spouse's vantage point. What creative solutions come to mind when you shift the focus from your spouse to what you could do differently?

2. Have you noticed any mood changes in your spouse lately? If so, pay attention to that change. Ask yourself, *Could this negative change in my spouse's attitude or mood be something caused by me?* Then discuss it with your spouse in an honest, calm manner and be open to any constructive criticism your spouse shares with you. Remember, your goal is to create a harmonious marriage. You have the rest of your lives to work out these issues with each other.

3. Do you and your spouse currently have a private "cue" to use with each other? If so, what is it? If not, discuss with your spouse the advantages of using a cue and what specific cue the two of you can begin using with each other to communicate discreetly when one of you unintentionally hurts the other's feelings.

FIVE WORDS OF PREVENTION

IF THERE IS SUCH A THING AS FIVE WORDS THAT CAN CHANGE your marriage—or at least how you communicate—they are quite possibly the ones contained in this powerful yet humbling phrase: "We should pray about that."

A few weeks ago I stumbled across an old interview in which Oprah asked Iyanla Vanzant, "What is your personal prayer?" In response, Iyanla gave three prayers she said will cover any situation: "Help!" "Help me now!" and "Thank you."[1] Thinking about that question for a moment, I don't know that I would have been able to answer it. "Thank you" is certainly the prayer I use most often. But when it comes to my marriage, if Keith and I aren't seeing eye to eye and he uses that five-word suggestion, my go-to prayer is very simple: "Am I wrong here? How do I quickly make it right?"

To this day, I don't recall how this began. I can't quite remember how I stumbled across this surefire way to prevent arguments. This much I do remember. Keith and I were having a conversation, and he was absolutely certain his point of view was correct.

I was rather certain it was not. My thought was we could do one of two things: either agree to disagree or continue expressing each other's sides until one agreed with the other. Only I was a bit tired of trying to get him to see my side as clearly as I saw it, and at the moment, he didn't seem too interested. Out of nowhere came this suggestion: "Honey, I think you should pray about that."

A GREAT "ARGUMENT PREVENTER"

In the marriage journal we wrote for my sister, Christy Joy, Keith mentioned this particular tip:

> Truth be told, I stole this little suggestion from Fawn and adopted it as my own. In the early stages of our relationship, we were having a discussion where I was so confident about the accuracy of my perceptions that I was unyielding. On this particular occasion I was winning the debate, or so I thought. . . .
>
> Enter the conversation showstopper and a great argument preventer. . . .
>
> Fawn calmly said, "You should pray about that." What do you do with that one? A neutral third party who happens to be God?
>
> It's a very powerful tool that shouldn't be misused. After all, what goes around comes around. Having said that, if you know that your spouse is wrong (or you think your spouse is wrong), directing him or her to prayer can only help matters. This phrase, when spoken in love, certainly makes it difficult to get upset, as it is so factual and indisputable.
>
> Typically, when I invoke the "prayer card" with Fawn,

I pray about it as well. Your goal should always be how you can attain a mutual understanding. If you can't do this by yourselves, there is no better way to reconcile the issue than with God.

When I shared this suggestion on Happy Wives Club, a marriage counselor commented that many men would not take too kindly to their wives telling them to pray about their viewpoints. That is why I changed the phrase to "We should pray about this," even though that is not what Keith and I personally use. Through the years, we've spoken to and treated each other with such respect that saying, "Honey, you should pray about that" hasn't offended or bothered him in the least. When he's made the same suggestion to me, I've just smiled, and sometimes even chuckled inside because it's the equivalent of using a trump card to win the match when playing bid whist.

Neither of us has ever been hurt or felt slighted by the suggestion to pray, and when it's been used, both of us have equally felt the responsibility to pray about it. We don't plan on changing the phrase we use, but saying "we" instead of "you" may sit better with you and your spouse. Go with whatever works best for you.

There are probably going to be times when you are certain your viewpoint is correct and your spouse just isn't "getting it." And there will undoubtedly be times when your spouse feels the same. For many people, their default in these situations is to argue their points so vigorously that the conversation begins to quickly accelerate out of control. Respect goes out the window and frustration takes over the driver's seat. The simple suggestion of having your spouse pray about a disagreeable point rather than allowing it to escalate has the power to preemptively end an argument before it has the opportunity to begin.

THE POWER OF FIVE SIMPLE WORDS

While writing on this topic, I asked two dear friends of ours, Byron and Annett, if they could remember an occasion in their twenty-three-year relationship (married eighteen of those years) when both were convinced their viewpoint was absolutely correct and needed to employ this strategy as an argument preventer. Almost as quickly as I asked the question, Byron chimed in, "What comes to mind immediately is the issue of homeschooling."

That surprised me. Not because homeschooling isn't a point of disagreement among many couples but rather because Annett is the biggest proponent of homeschooling I've ever met. Their children are absolutely brilliant. Whenever Keith and I are around them, we leave their presence in awe. Learning that Annett, the woman who has been a vocal supporter of homeschooling for the entire ten years we've known them, was strongly opposed to the idea at one point was a surprise, to say the least.

"It all began when we were dating," Byron continued. "I was competing for the US Swimming national team and traveling the world." He went on to share that in almost every country where he traveled, his host family homeschooled. Reinforced with nearly every visit to another country, the thought that home-schooling was the right way to educate his own children became cemented in his mind. After he and Annett were engaged, they began seriously discussing homeschooling as a possibility—or I should say Byron began discussing it as a possibility.

Annett wasn't interested in the least. They met at UCLA, where they both competed in sports. She'd gone to private school her entire life, both her parents were educators, their circle of friends and family were all educators, and homeschooling didn't have nearly as many options as it does today. She went on to excel at UCLA and then as a member of the USA Volleyball team, competing in the 2000 Summer Olympics. Byron went through the public school system before going to UCLA and then on to compete professionally in his sport, an additional bolster to Annett's viewpoint. There was just no way they were going to see eye to eye on this issue. That was, until the "showstopper" was introduced into the picture.

Instead of fighting the suggestion, Annett began researching the various curricula available. They even went to a homeschooling convention before their oldest son, Maya, was born. While researching, she discovered that people like Thomas Edison, Susan B. Anthony, Wolfgang Mozart, Florence Nightingale, Franklin D. Roosevelt, and Woodrow Wilson were all homeschooled.[2]

"It's hard for me to even think back and believe there was ever a time when I didn't support this," Annett added. She seemed to be amazed as Byron was recalling their discussions from two decades ago. Not that he wasn't relaying the information accurately but rather because she can't imagine her kids' lives any other way. "That seems like such a lifetime ago. I love it so much now!" she exclaimed. Having been around Annett, Byron, and their two children, I'm so happy they learned early the power in those five simple words: *We should pray about that.*

WHAT IF YOU DON'T PRAY?

While sharing this chapter with Keith, he said, "What about people who don't pray?" I must admit, I've traveled around the world interviewing couples who have mastered this principle of taking a "time-out," and each of them prayed. Whether Christian, Hindu, Buddhist, Muslim, or of any other faith, the point is they all prayed. Maybe you can't relate to this at all and might insert meditation here instead. I don't know if that will work, although I personally love daily meditation. Give it a try with whatever comes most naturally to you. What matters here is mutually agreeing to take a time-out and to pull back from your set opinions to focus on your spouse's viewpoints. The goal here is to keep a debate from turning into a heated argument.

THE BENEFITS OF ASKING
EACH OTHER TO PRAY

Debating an issue is fine, even good in many cases . . . until it goes downhill. And anyone married for longer than two weeks can probably attest that debates can go downhill very quickly if there aren't some safeguards in place. If I don't agree with something Keith says or vice versa, but it's important enough to one of us to continue the conversation instead of agreeing to disagree, rather than belaboring our own viewpoint, we usually ask each other to pray about it.

Will these five words all of a sudden make you the world's best communicator? Probably not. But they will invite an unbiased, nonpartisan person into the conversation who loves you both and will only tell you the truth—even when you are the one who is wrong.

And really, which of us doesn't need to be gently told sometimes that what we're absolutely certain about is not necessarily right and there is another way to look at it? We may not like it at the time, but like Annett, we'll be so happy when we can finally be of one accord.

———— *Day Seventeen Challenge Questions* ————

1. "We should pray about that." In what ways is this phrase a powerful argument preventer? How would these words bring perspective to discussions in which you and your spouse are each convinced you are right and are unyielding to the other's point of view?

2. What are the advantages of prayer when it comes to keeping a debate from turning into a heated argument? Why is it significant that *both* partners agree to pray about the issue? Or, if you aren't a person of prayer, what are the advantages of you and your spouse mutually agreeing to take a time-out from a debate to meditate, choosing to set aside your views for a few moments and focus on the other's?

3. "Anyone married for longer than two weeks can probably attest that debates can go downhill very quickly if there aren't some safeguards in place." How can this phrase—"We should pray about that"—become a safeguard in your marriage? Discuss this with your spouse. Agree together that when you and your spouse don't see eye to eye about something, you will calmly suggest that you both pray or meditate about the disagreeable point, rather than allowing it to escalate. Discover how these five little words have the power to end an argument before it begins.

KEEP A SCORELESS MARRIAGE

"DE-FENSE!" (STOMP, STOMP). "DE-FENSE! (STOMP, STOMP).

Christy Joy and I yelled at the top of our lungs while banging our feet on the bleachers. We were witnessing the game of a lifetime for Bishop Alemany High School. For the first time in the school's fifty-four-year history, the varsity boys' basketball team had made it to the CIF (California Interscholastic Federation) championships. More than twelve hundred fans had driven hours to see the game, the majority wearing cardinal-red T-shirts screened with the victory mantra "War Zone."

Our hearts were pounding, and we were losing our voices, but we had to keep cheering. Christy Joy's husband, Tray, was head coach of this basketball team. The support the fans displayed not only helped the team play better but warmed Tray's heart. Throughout the game we noticed a distinct difference between the times when our entire side of the stadium yelled, "De-fense!" (stomp, stomp) "De-fense!" (stomp, stomp), and the times when we did not. When we chanted in unison, the players jumped higher for rebounds, waved their hands aggressively in their competitors' faces, and ran like the floor was on fire. So we yelled like there was no tomorrow. Our goal was to motivate our players to keep the opposing team scoreless.

Our goal in screaming for defense against that opposing team has turned out to also be one of my greatest goals in marriage: to keep it scoreless. I've heard many people say, "Oh, I never keep score. If my spouse does something wrong, I forgive and move on." For most people saying that, it is absolutely true. Well, at least the "forgive and move on" part. But as I examined my heart a few years ago, I realized I kept score in a way most people may not even consider.

THREE WAYS TO KEEP SCORE IN MARRIAGE

There are actually three ways of keeping score in marriage. The first is to keep track of what your spouse does wrong, focusing on the error of his or her ways. The second is to keep track of everything you do right and expect a reciprocation of sorts. The third is to keep score against others' marriages. In all three cases, keeping score creates winners and losers.

1. Keeping Track of What Your Spouse Does Wrong

Early in our marriage I unintentionally kept score. As I mentioned in an earlier chapter, I didn't realize I was doing it, but every time Keith would point out an area of improvement for me, I'd immediately respond with something similar he did that also needed work. When I look back on that time, I am so disappointed in how I handled each of those opportunities for growth in my life. Instead of accepting his words immediately, I would defend myself.

I would eventually come around to considering what he

said—usually within a couple of hours—but my first response was often not right. I had a standing apology in place with him: "Honey, you know my first answer is usually not the right one, so please don't respond to that one and please wait for me to come back with the right response."

Thankfully, Keith knew my heart and always presumed innocence with me, so this standing apology bought me time for my poor answers without causing a dustup. Truly, grace in action. But what was causing my initial responses? The first and obvious cause was my pride and my desire to be perfect, a futile effort to say the least. But the second cause was my tendency to keep score. Subconsciously, every time Keith told me something I needed to do, I immediately responded with something he needed to do. Score one for the wife!

The problem with keeping score in this manner is that it was stifling my growth as a woman and wife. This man I loved, and whom I trusted more than anyone in the world, was trying to help me become a better person. And my first response was to push back. When we keep score, we hold on to something from the past and pull it to the present. In marriage, as well as in every other area of life, happiness and growth are in the now. The focus ahead is healthy and helpful. A focus on the past only takes you backward.

But even after I stopped keeping score by making sure I didn't keep a mental note of all Keith's shortcomings or everything he did wrong, I quickly realized my days as scorekeeper were far from over. A much more covert way of scorekeeping was still in the background.

2. Keeping Track of What You Do Right

This second way to keep score seems harmless but can be the most detrimental. I had stopped keeping track of when Keith did something wrong, but I was definitely keeping track of every time I did something right.

When I'd take out the trash instead of waiting for Keith to do it, count that as one point for me. When I cleaned up the house or did laundry even when my workdays were as jam-packed as his, I'd look for a gold star. I didn't realize this until several years into our marriage. When I did something, I wanted his recognition. When I was deciding on doing something I knew he'd appreciate but would be inconvenient for me, I often took inventory of what I'd most recently done and made my decision from there. I'm sure I don't need to tell you how flawed a thought process this is in marriage. As the saying goes, "Marriage is not 50–50; that's divorce. Marriage is 100–100. You have to give it everything you've got."

To overcome this second way of keeping score, I began reminding myself daily that all I give to my husband is just that, a gift. All I do for our household is not only for him but also for me. I had been treating my scorekeeping habit as something benign, but I had to stop kidding myself. "Gold star for Fawn" was the big joke in the house every time I did something for him or for us outside of my normal routine. It took me a few years, but I finally realized that keeping a scoreless marriage meant both not keeping score of what my husband did wrong and not keeping score of what I did right.

3. Keeping Track of What Other Couples Are Doing

The third way of keeping score, and quite possibly the one that trips most women up, is a tendency to keep score against other marriages. John bought Sally a new car for her birthday, always mows the lawn, and cooks and helps with housework.

Score one for the Johnsons! David always opens the car door for Anne, puts his arm around her whenever they're sitting down, and strokes her hand whenever he has a chance. Score one for the Smiths! Look at the amazing vacation Adam and Tracy took. Those pictures on Facebook are stunning. Score one for the Andersons!

Whether we realize it or not, if we aren't careful, this third way of keeping score can creep into any marriage. I published an article on the danger of comparisons not long ago, and the responses were quite telling. This kills so many marriages. Instead of focusing on the beauty of all you have, you focus on what you don't have. You spend much of your energy looking at what is lacking instead of breathing life into what you already have.

You Are What You Think

The founder of Ford Motor Company, Henry Ford, once said, "Whether you think you can or you think you can't, you're right." In marriage we have a similar choice in regard to our thoughts. We can produce good energy by saying positive things about marriage, building up our spouses, giving our all to the relationship, and not wasting any energy on keeping score.

Alternatively, we can produce negative energy by sowing seeds of doubt about whether what we have is enough. We can diminish the relationship and our love by choosing not to give our all or by keeping a mental note of it every time we do. We can tear down our spouses and our relationships by holding mistakes against our spouses, in public or in private.

How you think and what you believe will dictate the amount of time and energy you put into anything. Whether you think your spouse is or isn't the best person in the world for you, you are right. Whether you believe an argument-free marriage is possible or you determine it is not, you are right. Whether you trust positive actions will build a more solid love or if you decide they will not, you are right.

Someone once said, "You make a living from what you get. You make a life from what you give." This statement reflects the cyclical nature of giving. What you give is what you will receive. You must focus on giving the best of yourself, at all times, and trust that your spouse will do the same.

I love the way marriage author Alisa Bowman put it after realizing she'd also been keeping score: "In any relationship, happiness never comes from keeping a mental tally of who does more of what. Happiness comes from asking for support when you need it, from letting go of the small stuff, and from championing your spouse when he wants an atta boy for cooking the last quarter of a meal."[1]

Rather than keeping score when your spouse does something wrong, apply grace. Instead of keeping score when you do something right, remind yourself that everything you give will be returned to you in abundance, although maybe not in that exact moment. As I'm sure you've already experienced in every other area of your life, what you give is like a boomerang: it will come back. And the next time you think about keeping score against another marriage, remind yourself that you have the ability to create the marriage of your dreams every day. Remember also that your dream marriage should not replicate any other. That would be quite boring and unoriginal, don't you think?

ONE SCORE TO CONSIDER

A couple of years ago I asked my husband two questions I highly recommend you ask your spouse. I should, however, add this disclaimer. When I posed the first question, Keith's answer initially crushed my spirit. But I assure you, the crushing was well worth it. His honest and transparent response made me a better woman, friend, and wife.

What's the question that crushed me and yet I still recommend you ask your spouse? Here it is:

> ON A SCALE OF 1 TO 10, WITH 10 REPRESENTING THE SPOUSE YOU BELIEVE I HAVE THE POTENTIAL TO BE, HOW WOULD YOU RANK ME TODAY?

Before asking this question, there is something incredibly important to consider. You have to create a welcoming environment for your spouse to give his or her most honest response. If you can do that, this one question may be the catalyst that takes your marriage from good to great or from great to extraordinary.

If you've read *Happy Wives Club*, you know I wasn't prepared for such an honest answer. My husband has always been great at pointing out all the wonderful things about me. He's complimented me so often throughout our marriage that I had no idea how much room I still had to grow. Honestly, I was expecting a score of 9+. I knew he wouldn't give me a 10, because we all have room to grow. But I thought for sure he would rate me a 9.

When he began his response with, "Compared to so-and-so, on a scale of 1 to 10, you're a 100," I knew his score, and the one I thought he'd give me, were unlikely to match. My score when I posed this question to him in 2012, nine years into our marriage? He gave me a soft 7.

I know that might not seem horrible to most of you, but as a former GM of a Hilton-branded hotel, in which all customer service scores of 8 or below were calculated as 0, it was a mighty big pill to swallow. His rationale for the score made me feel a bit better: "If I compared you to anyone else in the world, you'd be a 10. But you asked me to compare you to the wife you have the potential to be." Even with that explanation, I was still disappointed. But I've never regretted asking that question. Nor have I regretted posing this follow-up question:

CAN YOU GIVE ME A LIST OF SIX THINGS I CAN DO TO BECOME A BETTER SPOUSE?

Let me tell you, this question is golden. Here are two things this question does:

1. It shows your spouse that you care so much about your marriage that no matter how great it already is, you want it to be better.
2. It causes your spouse to think about and appreciate all the things you already do right.

For fun, while you're waiting for your spouse to give you that list of six things (it took my husband two days and a gentle reminder), try writing your own list of twelve things you think will be on his or her list. This exercise was a huge eye-opener for me. Of the twelve things I'd included on my list, only one was actually on his. The six things he gave me were minor tweaks I could do easily. But what he was looking for was consistency.

For me and my marriage, this practice was a game changer.

———————— *Day Eighteen Challenge Questions* ————————

1. In what ways have you been "keeping score" in your marriage? Review the list of three types of scorekeeping common in marriage relationships. Do you tend to keep track of what your spouse does wrong? If so, rather than pointing out things your spouse needs to work on, choose to apply grace. Have you been keeping score of what you are doing right in your marriage and expecting your spouse's approval? If so, change your perspective to embrace the reality that everything you give to your spouse is just that—a gift that you give freely in the context of a loving, gracious union.

2. Do you tend to compare your marriage to other people's relationships? Does scrolling through your news feed on social media or listening to your friends talk about their marriages fill you with envy? If you are keeping score about what other couples are doing, remember that every day you and your spouse have the ability to create the unique marriage of your dreams.

3. Sit down with your spouse and ask each other the following two questions:

   • "On a scale of 1 to 10, with 10 representing the spouse you believe I have the potential to be, what would you rank me today?"
   • "Can you give me a list of six things I can do to become a better spouse?"

4. These questions, when asked in a welcoming environment, will help you create a scoreless marriage—and they may well be the catalyst that takes your marriage from good to extraordinary.

SIMPLIFY YOUR LIFE

IF YOU ENTERED THE FAMILY ROOM OF OUR HOME, YOU'D SEE a wooden sign that sits on top of our coffee table. The plaque reads, "Simplify." It is our daily reminder that no matter how complicated life becomes, our home and our family are to remain simple. There are parts of this life we cannot simplify, such as work, government, war, poverty, sickness, and disease. But there are some areas we have the ability and power to simplify, such as our home and our marriage.

YOUR HOME, YOUR REFUGE

Keith and I determined years ago that we'd make our home a place of refuge from the world. No matter what happened at work or elsewhere, home would be our place of calm. There is a song by Rascal Flatts called "Mayberry," which I love to sing while driving in the car. That song transports me to a complication-free place and time, a world of total serenity, where my biggest worry is running out of ice-cold Cherry Coke or not knowing what whimsical shape the next cloud will take. Ah, I love that place. Every time I get to the chorus I smile from ear to ear.

But just as the song goes, "Sometimes it feels like this world is spinning faster than it did in the old days," my iPhone rings. It's my assistant; there's an urgent request. Then my iPhone begins buzzing; the article an online news outlet previously needed by Monday is now needed on Friday to be published on Monday. Of course, today is Friday.

I have a dinner with family at six, so I'd better leave by four. The restaurant is only twenty-five minutes away, but with the Los Angeles traffic—the drivers honking, swerving in and out of lines, and texting at the same time—I'd better get on the road soon. How in the world can I finish the article on time but still leave on time? High stress. Extreme frustration. And so my visions of the simple life end around the same time as the song does.

When did our lives become so complicated? Do you remember when yours went from calm to chaotic? I don't remember the exact moment in my life, but something tells me it involved the introduction of the BlackBerry, iPhone, or other devices that have been my constant companions for the past twenty years. If the introduction of the smartphone wasn't enough, texting, instant messaging, and social networking sites like Facebook make us accessible to almost anyone who would like to reach us at any time.

Most of us have discovered that our lives are more complicated than we ever imagined they could be, and we are trying to figure out how to get back to a simpler time. Maybe your life was never simple, so you're just hoping to get there one day. Well, I can't help you with the complications of work or traffic, but perhaps I can help you with a few aspects of marriage.

COMPLICATED LIVES LEAD TO
CONTENTIOUS MARRIAGES

As you know, Keith and I have spent quite a bit of time studying other couples. Some come to us asking for advice, and others we watch as examples of marriages that flourish or falter. When a couple is struggling, we listen intently to try and understand the reason for their challenges. Overwhelmingly, the couples with the most contentious marriages are also the ones with the most complicated lives outside of the home. These couples allow life's stresses to enter the family territory. There is so much outside of our control, but what happens in our home and marriage is certainly within our realm of influence.

The marital complications we see most often include keeping up appearances for family, friends, and neighbors by purchasing fancy cars, houses, and clothing while secretly struggling financially. Choosing to keep past flames as a part of the family's inner circle, thereby failing to permanently close the door on a former romantic relationship, is also high on the list.

Do any of these sound familiar? In-laws, stepchildren, infertility, extended family, money woes, long work hours, poor salaries—all these stresses can weigh heavily on our shoulders. There comes a time when we need to sit down and figure out which ones we have the ability to influence and which ones we do not. Each of us faces different complications in life, and simplifying as many of those complications as possible is one of the keys in the pursuit of an argument-free marriage.

SIMPLIFY YOUR LIFE BY SAYING NO

Keith and I have made a commitment to live a simplified life, at least as much as is in our control. We apply this principle to every aspect of our life, including family, friends, and finances. That means that we say no to attending events and family gatherings every week. No to lending money we can't afford not to get back. No to certain volunteer opportunities and church activities. No to friends stopping by on days we've designated as a time of rest.

We calendar our dates like a million-dollar meeting. "Sorry, we can't join you for that, as we already have something on our calendar," is something we find ourselves saying often. And it is 100 percent true. There is something on our calendar: *Us time.* I learned this last year from a couple I interviewed in Australia. For decades, they've had "Date Night" on their calendar every Wednesday. When they get requests to go somewhere or do something else at that time, they immediately respond with, "We can't. We're booked." If you had a million-dollar business idea and had a meeting scheduled with an investor who could make it happen, would you ever consider canceling it? That's how you should treat this time with your spouse. Once it's on the calendar, nothing short of an emergency of catastrophic proportions should cause you to cancel it.

Having the ability to lend others money is great. But if you are overextending yourself to help others, to the point that it is hurting your marriage, this is an area in which to begin saying no. Saying no is not always easy, but in order to simplify your lives, you have to become comfortable with that finite, monosyllabic word.

Today's challenge is simple: In what areas can you begin saying no in order to simplify your life?

——— Day Nineteen Challenge Questions ———

1. In what ways is your life today more complicated than you ever imagined it could be? Think back to five, or even ten, years ago. What stressors are you dealing with now that you didn't have back then? How have these additional stress factors affected your life—and your marriage?

2. "There is so much outside of our control, but what happens in our home and marriage is certainly within our realm of influence." What stressors have you allowed into your family territory that do not belong in your marriage? For example, excessive spending to keep up appearances for others, maintaining contact with former romantic partners, bringing work issues home, and so forth. What steps can you take today to remove each of these stress factors from your home?

3. In what areas can you and your spouse begin saying no in order to simplify your life? Reducing your stress level by simplifying your life as much as possible is essential to a harmonious, argument-free marriage.

HONOR YOUR FAMILY

"YOU MUST BE PRESENT FOR EVERY CHRISTMAS, Thanksgiving, birthday, school play, clarinet recital, and soccer game in our kids' lives. I want you to love them and spoil them and teach them things that Kevin and I can't. Like how to throw a right hook, for example."[1] In the 2005 hit movie *Monster-in-Law*, Viola, a meddling future mother-in-law played by Jane Fonda, reluctantly receives these words from her soon-to-be daughter-in-law, Charlie, played by Jennifer Lopez.

After months of sabotaging the relationship between her son and his fiancée, Charlie, Viola finally "wins" and Charlie agrees to call off the wedding, just moments before the bride and groom are scheduled to head down the aisle. In the one touching scene of the movie, Viola comes to her senses and asks Charlie not to call off the wedding and destroy her son's happiness. Viola agrees to some rules and boundaries, and in exchange Charlie invites her mother-in-law to be a part of their family life.

If only this movie were an exaggeration of the relationship between many in-laws and the person their son or daughter has chosen to marry. A study released in Malaysia in 2009 found, "Interference by in-laws is the main reason for Indians to divorce. It is the top-ranked reason at 30 percent."[2] In Western countries, we may not be able to imagine in-laws being the top reason for divorce, but they very well may be one of the top reasons for arguments.

According to a psychologist at the University of Cambridge, 60 percent of daughters-in-law felt that friction with their husband's mother had caused them long-term stress.[3]

HONOR YOUR SPOUSE FIRST

I know few people who have as much fun as our friends Ray and Lucia. For years they've backpacked throughout the world. Quite frankly, they're far more adventurous than Keith and me, as they will go to another country with not so much as a reservation. As I write this, they are in Brazil for the World Cup. They'll work for a few years, save enough money to take a month's vacation from work, and then somehow make their money stretch across three continents. They stay in hostels, pitch tents, or share homes with friendly people they meet on the streets in other countries. We love living vicariously through them. They are like *The Amazing Race* without cameras in tow.

When their son was born, they resolved to continue traveling and to make sure their marriage came first in the family dynamic. Date night is a ritual at least once a week. Their son stays with family while Mommy and Daddy have some alone time. Lucia is of Latin heritage and Ray is Italian. Both have families who pride themselves in being heavily involved in the raising of the *entire* family, including grandchildren. But because of their love for each other and the relationship they forged from the beginning, no one dares step between them or say anything unkind to one about the other. They are a united front as husband and wife and as parents.

When it comes to children, I will give little advice because, as you know, Keith and I have been unable to have them. But I do interact with thousands of Happy Wives Club members each day, and the majority of them have children. I've spent the past few years interviewing couples happily married more than twenty-five years, and other than a few outliers, they have all raised children or are now raising them.

The piece of advice mentioned most is to make sure the relationship with your spouse comes first and foremost. It seems easier said than done, but according to the couples who make this recommendation, the dividends earned in both your marriage and the relationship with your children will be worth the effort.

James and Meg were only married a few years before their son Aaron came into the picture. Two years later, their second son, Anderson, was born. And three years later, a daughter, Maggie. For nearly twenty-four years, Meg was consumed with raising the children. Soccer practice, Little League baseball games, school plays, homework, and parent-teacher conferences took up most of her days. Before she knew it, her kids were graduating from college and leaving the house to establish their own homes. An emptiness set in as Meg discovered she barely knew the man she'd shared a bed with for the past twenty-five years.

While Meg was busy giving all her attention to Aaron, Maggie, and Anderson, she had been neglecting her relationship with James. She never noticed that he had begun staying late at work and putting in long hours. He knew his colleagues would appreciate his work at the office and would reward him with pats on the back. This recognition was something he never seemed to receive from Meg and the kids. So they lived separate lives under one roof. After the kids moved out, Meg became very depressed. She'd invested everything in her children, and now they'd moved on with their lives.

This scenario happens in households all over the world. Husbands and wives become parents and forget to keep their relationship first; they neglect to ensure that when the children grow up, their marriage will not grow apart. Top relationship and parenting experts agree that it is necessary for the relationship between the parents to be solid and to be stronger than the bond with their child. I don't know a parent who would not give everything up, even die, for his or her child. But our relationships with our spouses must be even stronger than that.

HONOR YOUR CHILDREN SECOND

Whenever this topic comes up, I always think back to my first interaction with Miriam. Keith and I have become close friends with not only Efi and her but also their grown children. And although we continue to learn from them every time we get together, it is still the frank and practical yet simple advice she gave in our first encounter that I return to on this subject. During our time together, I asked her why she believed marriages in the United States fail at such a disproportionately high rate compared to those in most of the world. "Common sense!" she responded.

When I asked her to elaborate on what she meant, she said, "I believe in the basics. My attitude is this: I'm not going to reinvent the wheel. Family must come first. And when I say family, I mean your spouse must come before all else, next your children, and after that your parents."

I asked what she noticed as the main differences between marriages she'd observed around the world throughout her travels and those in the United States. Responding without hesitation, she said, "The others are more family oriented." She told me that in her Israeli culture it is not uncommon for the entire family to meet for dinner each night to discuss their days and to relax—together. It is also a common belief that one's spouse comes before the children, so that's the order in which attention should be given. Spouse first. Children second. Period.

I inquired why she thought it was so difficult for many Americans to put their spouses first. "For so long women have been taught that children are to come first," she said. "It began with the feminist movement, which, albeit with good intentions, taught us to put ourselves and our children first in everything. We're taught that kids are everything. You hear women say they'd die for their children. But their children were not the first ones to come along. Just as we would not pack up our children and leave them on the front porch if they did something we didn't like, we should not consider doing this to our spouses."

I love an e-mail I received from another member of the Happy Wives Club, who has been married for sixty-five years. "I think it is truly remarkable in these times to be so happily married for so long. In addition, following our example, all three of our children are incredibly happy: two couples for forty-one years, and our baby and her spouse for thirty years. I think the best gift parents can give their children is to allow them to observe every single day how fantastically marvelous love and marriage can be."

What an honor to be able to create love and peace in your home for the life of your children. Rather than listening to a couple argue and believing it is par for the course, your children will know it isn't necessary. Your children will not find it peculiar or unusual to spend more time laughing, playing, and enjoying each other than fighting, storming around the house, and slamming doors.

These couples gave their children the greatest gift possible. They created a new kind of normal that resulted in a marriage that flourishes in the good times and in the bad, in sickness and in health, till death do them part.

HONOR YOUR PARENTS AND IN-LAWS THIRD

In a magazine article I read years ago, a reader wrote in with the question, "What do you do if you don't get along with your mother-in-law to-be, and what is the best way to tell your significant other?" To that, the writer responded by pointing out—in a far more matter-of-fact tone than I will use here—it is utter foolishness to tell your spouse that you don't like the woman who gave birth to him or her and subsequently raised them to be the person you chose to marry.

She then went on to remind the reader that the commandment to honor your father and mother included in-laws. It would be torturous to force your spouse to choose between the woman who birthed him or her, and you. And it always has grave consequences for everyone involved. Whether she's earned your respect or not, she deserves it. She deserves it because without her, your spouse would not be your spouse.

Years later, that question and the magazine writer's response have stayed with me. No matter how crazy your in-laws may seem, they are your spouse's parents. Don't force your spouse to choose between you and the parents he or she loves. I know this might be difficult, especially if your in-laws are not the loving and accepting type, but give it a try. Your efforts to bring peace to the family in this way can only strengthen the relationship between you and your spouse.

That being said, when a man and a woman are married, they enter into a bond that supersedes all other relationships. Your relationship must always come first, then your relationship with the children, and then the in-laws. I am blessed to have fantastic in-laws whom I cherish. They don't meddle in our relationship and are happy their son married someone he adores and who loves him exceedingly in return.

FOR THOSE WITH AN IN-LAW CHALLENGE

If your relationship with your in-laws is fabulous, feel free to skip this section. For those needing a little encouragement in this area, continue here.

Every day I post positive quote memes on marriage on the Happy Wives Club Facebook page. Not long ago I posted one that read, "To my mother-in-law, thank you for raising the love of my life." It was shared by almost twenty thousand people. That got me to thinking, *I bet the women of this club have some great tips for building a relationship with your in-laws.* So a few mornings later, I posed the question, "If you get along well with your in-laws, what would you say has been the key to building that relationship?"

More than five hundred people responded and provided us with some great tips. If I could quickly sum up what seemed to make the most difference, it was BRAWL: Boundaries, Respect,

Acceptance, Willingness, and Love. So instead of having a "brawl" with your in-laws, as so many unfortunately do, remember that they helped make your spouse who he or she is and try creating *boundaries*, giving *respect*, *accepting* them as they are, showing a *willingness* to consider things from their point of view, and *loving* them no matter what because without them, your spouse would not be your spouse.

—————— *Day Twenty Challenge Questions* ——————

1. Do you and your spouse have children? If so, how can you begin today to make your relationship with each other as husband and wife a priority over your parenting? Take a look at your family calendar. Are you spending more time shuttling kids to activities than you are spending time with your spouse? Consider what adjustments you might need to make to your routine to create a strong bond with your spouse.

2. How does cultivating a healthy, happy marriage give your children "the greatest gift possible"? Describe some of the benefits children experience in a home filled with peace and love, built on a marriage that flourishes in the good times and in the bad.

3. How would you describe your relationship with your parents and your in-laws? If you are struggling in either of these relationships, implement the principle of BRAWL: Boundaries, Respect, Acceptance, Willingness, and Love. Discuss with your spouse ways you can create *boundaries*, give *respect*, *accept* them as they are, show a *willingness* to consider things from their point of view, and *love* them no matter what.

BEGIN WITH THE
END IN MIND

In the spring of 2014, I ran a series on my blog entitled "The Best Marriage Advice I've Ever Received." Then I invited four of my favorite bloggers to share the best marriage advice they had ever received. Maggie Reyes was one of the four, and so was Christine St. Vil. After I asked Christine for her response, she tried to think back to her wedding video and all the words of wisdom shared by her guests, but nothing really came to mind. Then she thought back to her bridal shower and the seven years she and her husband dated before finally saying "I do," and nothing stuck out.

She began racking her brain for things she'd learned throughout all the interviews she'd done with married couples and couldn't think of a single thing. Then, after running every marriage-related piece of advice she'd ever received through her head, one thing shone like a light from above, and it came from her parents, who'd been married forty-seven years:

The only end goal you should have in marriage is to honor, love, and cherish each other until the day you die.

The only way for two spouses to honor, love, and cherish each other for life is to understand that marriage was not designed solely for your own benefit. When you understand this, tensions may arise but they don't last very long.

I gladly work through my obstacles and challenges in my marriage because I know that those moments are just that . . . moments. They don't define our marriage. They only make our marriage stronger and allow us to work more fluidly together as a unit.

Beginning with the end in mind means that we may not agree on an issue today or tomorrow. But we have a lifetime together to make it work. It means that there are days we'll make each other really happy, and there will be days where we may not even want to talk to each other. It means that there will be days when we can't keep our hands off of each other and days where we don't even want to touch.

But there will be so many more days that we spend joking, laughing, cuddling, and hugging. Those are the days that we choose to focus on because those are the days that allow us to focus with the end in mind.

Beginning with the end in mind means that we are working toward one goal—together. It means that we're in this marriage journey together, as one unit.

Beginning with the end in mind allows you to thrive in turbulent times. Team this with having "no plan B," and there is no question you have what it takes to create an argument-free marriage.

A Long-Term Perspective on Obstacles

"What is the biggest obstacle you've had to overcome in your marriage and how did you do it?"

This was the question posed to Keith and me during a recent interview. You would think that might be an easy question to answer, right? Well, not for us. In every interview we've done together, this question has caused us a bit of discomfort because we know what the interviewer is looking for but we don't have it to give.

The truth is, we've never had a challenge in our marriage that has felt, well, major. Granted, we went through a failed adoption after we'd spent months planning our new life, putting the crib together, and rolling around on plush carpets in the local hardware store to pick the perfect one for our new baby. An experience like that might tear some families apart. I've seen that happen. And yes, most couples consider infertility a major challenge.

At a New Year's Eve event last year, I spent a great deal of time speaking with two ladies. They were fascinated by the Happy Wives Club and wanted to know what would make someone actually begin such a thing. As I began to explain, one of the ladies became more and more intrigued. As it turned out, she was in the middle of a divorce from a man she believed to be her soul mate and best friend. She spoke about him as if he was the most wonderful person to ever grace this earth. What could possibly tear apart two people who were this much in love? Infertility. She'd always dreamed of being a mother, and they learned, after they were married, that he could not have children. Infertility, for many, is a deal breaker. And if not that, it is at the very least a great strain.

For Keith and me, infertility is just another challenge we've faced together. We continue to be filled with gratitude that our insurance covers the majority of fertility procedures, and we consider our childless eleven years together an opportunity to grow closer as husband and wife.

Aside from infertility and a failed adoption, yes, there have been other difficulties in our lives, but none that felt like real obstacles. None that caused us to pull away from each other rather than team up togeher to overcome the challenge. It wasn't until a similar question was posed during a talk I was giving to a group of financial advisers earlier this year that I had an *aha* moment about this issue.

"We hear that money problems are the number one reason for divorce. Based on the stats, of course, we know that is not true," an audience member said. "Can you explain why this adversely affects some marriages and not others?"

In answering that question, I finally realized why Keith and I have such a hard time answering that "obstacle" question. I began:

Have you ever been on an airplane going through major turbulence? The kind that feels like the plane is dropping several hundred feet at a time? On a recent flight, the plane was dropping at such steep rates that with each drop almost every passenger on the flight gasped.

A young man, no older than thirty, sitting next to me was sweating so profusely that he looked as if he had just finished a spinning class. With every drop in altitude, you could almost see his heart popping out of his chest. I'm telling you, that young man thought he was about to die.

But then I turned around and looked at the flight attendants, and it was as if they were on a completely different plane.

"Trash anyone?" was their call down the middle of the aisle. "Can I take that cup from you, sir?" was the flight attendant's question to a man who was probably clutching his cup for dear life.

These flight attendants were utterly unfazed. They were going through the exact same turbulence as the rest of us, and yet it was as if they were flying through clear, sunny skies. There, of course, is a simple reason for that. They knew that the odds of a fatality happening on that plane were one in ten million. They'd been through similar turbulence more times than they could count.

This is the difference between the couples who allow finances, infertility, and other similar challenges to adversely affect their marriages and the ones who don't. Those who look ahead to the future, team up, and work to overcome life's challenges together are like the flight attendants on that plane. They're going through the same tumultuous airspace as everyone else, but they remain focused on what they know to be true: they will make it through.

Every person on this planet goes through turbulent skies at some point. But if your union has love, respect, faith, and trust—and if you begin with the end in mind—you can protect your marriage from the turbulence of life. By coming together and supporting each other, remembering that those rocky skies are just for a moment, you can draw closer rather than be pulled apart. Your love, just like that plane, is far more powerful than any turbulence you might endure.

Challenging times are for the moment. Your beautiful, unique union is for a lifetime. That is, if you will begin today with the end in mind.

—————— *Day Twenty-One Challenge Questions* ——————

1. In your own words, explain what it means to "begin with the end in mind" in your marriage. How could this principle affect your perspective on things that are frustrating you or causing you stress? What effects could this perspective have on the way you communicate with your spouse? Be specific.

2. What is the biggest obstacle you've faced in your marriage so far? Using the principle of "begin with the end in mind," take a moment to redefine that obstacle. How important is that obstacle in light of the many years you will spend with your spouse? Zoom out to consider that you and your spouse have an entire lifetime together. How does this big-picture view affect your perspective on any challenges you have faced or are currently facing?

3. In what ways would beginning with the end in mind help you and your spouse become more unified in your marriage goals? Discuss with your spouse how this approach could strengthen your marriage and help both of you thrive in turbulent times.

WEEK FOUR

THE NUMBER ONE
REASON FOR STRIFE

ROBIN AND MICHAEL LIVED A GREAT LIFE IN A LARGE HOUSE
on a cul-de-sac at the base of a gorgeous mountain. Everything
about their life seemed charmed, but they had a secret they were
keeping from most of their friends and family. They were going
broke.

Robin was a successful entrepreneur who, for three million dollars, sold her interest in a company she founded. No
sooner had the ink on the deal dried than Robin and Michael
decided to upgrade their lifestyle. They already had a lovely
home, but they wanted a larger one with a pool, media room,
and more space.

During the first few years, they threw lavish pool par-
ties and hosted events for every major holiday for family and
friends, including Keith and me, whom they didn't know well
but still invited. Robin was a huge fan of expensive couture and
beauty treatments, so she continued this in the years following

the sale of her business. After the sale, however, Robin no longer had an income, and their lifestyle required much more than Michael's mid-level executive salary. Their fairy-tale life began to unravel quickly once they welcomed twin boys into the world and Michael was tasked with being the sole breadwinner of the home.

After they'd spent the money from the sale of Robin's business, the couple's arguments began to increase in frequency and intensity. Michael was upset that Robin did not curtail her spending after the kids were born but instead spent more. Robin hurled insults at Michael for his poor handling of their finances and didn't appreciate his hypocritical and condescending comments regarding her spending. Clearly he enjoyed showing off his fancy watches, cars, and their house. They held it together as long as they could before filing for bankruptcy. Not long after that, divorce papers were signed.

THE STRESS OF FINANCIAL CHALLENGES

For the past thirty or so years, finances have consistently appeared in the top three or four reasons for divorce cited by US couples. The stress of financial challenges seems to cause arguments with more frequency than any other issue. If you haven't experienced financial issues in your marriage yet, that's wonderful. I'd rather you have the information and not need it than need the information and not have it. Much of what I learned in my twelve weeks of premarital counseling I never thought I'd need to use. But man oh man, am I happy I was paying attention, because when storms have come our way, we've been able to dance in the rain.

MAKE A DECISION TO BECOME
DEBT-FREE TOGETHER

At the start of the Great Recession, Keith and I made the decision to work as a team toward becoming debt-free. Financial analysts were predicting the United States was headed for its second depression, and Keith and I concluded it was the perfect time to begin working toward financial freedom. Companies were laying off people by the thousands, and we realized being dependent on either one of our employers for our livelihood—both of whom were downsizing at the time—would not be wise for our family's future. Around the same time, Keith stumbled across a fantastic book by author Dave Ramsey called *The Total Money Makeover*. It completely changed the way we viewed, spent, and saved our money.

Early in our marriage we made a commitment to each other to pursue as simple a life as possible while maintaining our drive and desire to succeed in every aspect of our lives. Striving for a simple life meant we would need to learn to wear our possessions lightly, meaning we would need to be willing to quickly shed whatever belongings could eventually cause us stress.

THE BEST THINGS IN LIFE
REQUIRE SACRIFICE

Our friends David and Linda were faced with making this decision during the economic downturn of 2008. But instead of shedding their possessions willingly, they held on to them until they were finally forced by creditors to let it all go. David was a big spender. They both made good money, and he wanted everyone to know it.

Linda was far less impressed by material things and wished David would save rather than spend. She told him regularly how much his spending could get them in trouble if for some reason he ever lost his job. And then it happened: his company downsized, and David was laid off.

Within three months their bank account was nearly empty, and David found that most of his purchases (watches, cars, clothes) weren't worth much used. Linda cried, frustrated and hurt, when they had to pack up their bags and leave their family, friends, and lives behind to head to Texas, where David's new job was located and where they could afford to live on lower salaries. Although they made it through this period with their family intact, it was an extremely rough time, taking a toll on their marriage and their children.

We must make difficult decisions throughout life, especially when it comes to marriage and family. The best way to handle finances is certainly one of the toughest choices you will make. By simplifying them, however, you just might find the peace that has eluded your home for so many years.

Don't Be a Part of the 70 Percent

Recently I came across the newest edition of *Money* magazine. On the cover was a large image of two one-hundred-dollar bills positioned on their sides with the bottoms touching and the tops slightly turned in to create two curves along the top. Two Benjamins turned into a singular heart shape with the cover story title: "Couples + Money: 7 Ways to Grow Richer Together."

In the article, *Money* shared the results of a recent nation-wide survey of one thousand married adults. Much of the article focused on the shift in households from men being the only bread-winners to "women in dual-earner households now bring[ing] in about half of the family income and nearly a quarter of wives earn[ing] more than their husbands." Debunking the myth that marriages in which the woman makes more are prone to more fighting, have lousy sex lives, or are more prone to divorce seemed to be the overarching storyline. As the article stated, "The problem with these characteristics? They're not necessarily accurate."[1]

The article went on to explain that the reports that husbands suffer from bruised egos and feelings of emasculation when they make less are based on data from couples interviewed in the early to mid-1990s, "missing a generation's worth of shifting expectations and experience when it comes to working women and marriage."

Although much of the article focused on that shifting cultural landscape, what caught my attention were two specific results. The first was that "70 percent of married couples argue about money—ahead of fights about household chores, togetherness, sex, snoring and what's for dinner."

REDUCE ARGUMENTS BY
SORTING OUT FINANCES

For years, many people have stated that the number one reason for divorce is finances, but research has never backed that up. What research has said time and time again, however, is that married couples argue more about money than anything else. Because I have known this for many years, helping couples sort out their finances has been something it's been my honor to do. Not as an expert, but as someone who partnered with her spouse to create financial freedom during the worst recession since the 1930s. I don't purport to know the only way to create financial freedom in your marriage. As a matter of fact, if I searched for books on that subject, I could probably find hundreds available right now. So please know there are many step-by-step programs out there dedicated to assisting you in becoming financially free, and I recommend searching for one that appeals to you most.

What you will find in this final week of our twenty-eight-day challenge isn't a step-by-step plan for alleviating debt, although the pages that follow will certainly help. My focus in this final week is sharing how you and your spouse, if it is your desire, can maintain your love and commitment toward each other, even in the midst of a financial crisis.

FIVE AGREEMENTS THAT LEAD TO
FEWER ARGUMENTS ABOUT FINANCES

As we continue this final week of this twenty-eight-day argument-free challenge, there are five essential foundational beliefs that you should know about:

1. Finances do not dictate the happiness in your marriage. You do. Lasting happiness in marriage is like happiness in anything else. It must be chosen, deliberately, and on a moment-by-moment basis. This doesn't mean you won't feel the stress or strain. It's real. It can be tough. And it's all right. What matters is that you team up together to defeat the foe—debt and financial challenges—rather than turning on each other. As Zig Ziglar said, "Many marriages would be better if the husband and wife clearly understood they are on the same side."[2]

2. Managing finances is a joint task. As confirmed by research over the years, and as recently as this week by the *Money* survey I

referenced earlier, "it makes sense to delegate money management to the person who is more interested, better organized, or more frugal. Both research and anecdotal evidence shows that couples should not make a decision about which one controls the finances based on income or gender, and that whoever makes the financial decisions should consult with their spouse."[3] In our household, Keith or I could do it, as we are equally skilled at it, so although Keith manages our finances now, that could change next year and then change back to him a year after that.

3. Blaming causes procrastination. It is difficult to work on a problem we don't acknowledge we have the tools and ability to fix. When we spend time pointing fingers at anyone but ourselves, we prolong the inevitable: no progress. We all play a part in our personal financial situations, and we all hold the keys to change them for the better or for the worse. Beginning today, if you have not already, make a commitment to stop pointing fingers. This is a team effort and can only be solved jointly and cooperatively.

4. If you spend more than you earn, you will perpetually be in debt. In May 2012, Rasmussen Reports released a survey for *Country Financial* with fascinating results. Of the three thousand respondents, about half said they spent more than they earned at least a few months each year. And yet, only 10 percent believed they were living above their means. In the following chapters, my assumption is we agree that if you spend more than you earn, that is one of the ways to get in debt—and reversing that pattern is one of the only ways to get out.

5. Credit cards should be used sparingly and paid off at the end of every month. Credit cards were never meant to be a form of income. They are great for convenience, but when they become a necessity and money that could be used for essentials is being wasted on interest, something's got to give. For those in credit card

debt, don't worry, we were there too, and we'll talk about how to overcome this.

If we can agree on these five points, or at the very least if you are willing to consider them, what lies beyond these initial pages just might be the key to ending the financially charged arguments and tensions in your home so you can work together as a team to create the life and marriage of your dreams.

—— Day Twenty-Two Challenge Questions ——

1. What percentage of your arguments with your spouse is related to your finances? Would you say this is an area you are currently struggling with? If you and your spouse committed together to follow the steps to financial freedom outlined in the next six days, what possible effects could that decision have on your marriage? Be specific.

2. Which spouse takes primary responsibility for managing the finances in your household? Is this arrangement currently working? If not, what changes could you make to your roles to make your finances run more efficiently? What steps will you take to make sure that both spouses know where the money is and have access to all account information?

3. Do you and your spouse have a monthly budget? If so, review your budget and make any adjustments necessary to prepare for your journey to financial freedom. If you don't have a budget, go to www.DaveRamsey.com and download "Dave's Budgeting Forms." Consider investing in Dave Ramsey's book *The Total Money Makeover* or attending a Financial Peace University class near you (http://www.daveramsey.com/fpu) and work through the financial principles together with your spouse. You'll be glad you did!

THE COMPARISON TRAP

I'M ECSTATIC YOU ARE STILL READING ON DAY TWENTY-THREE of this challenge. If you made it here, I'll add one more essential belief to the five I stated yesterday: there is a good chance a source of conflict in your marriage has been, to some degree, related to finances. I assume this because at some point, in almost every marriage, finances are an issue. Maybe you struggled with finances in the past. Maybe you're struggling right now. Or maybe your financial struggle lies somewhere in the future.

If you are currently having financial trouble, how long have you been in debt? And as long as we're being honest, how long were you in debt before you actually realized you were in debt? For my part, I remained in some form of debt most of my life. Even when I only had the ability to make minimum payments on my credit cards, I didn't think I was in debt.

After becoming debt-free (as most define it to exclude mortgages), Keith and I decided—against the advice of most financial advisors—to begin paying off our mortgage. We don't consider ourselves to be debt-free because of our mortgage, but we have made our household financially free, and I'll share with you the difference over the next few days. But for the purpose of this chapter, allow me to share with you a few thoughts:

1. Creating a financially free household—even if you've been struggling since the economy began sliding downhill (or even before)—is still possible, and you can begin today.

2. Securing financial freedom for your household requires not an individual effort but a team effort, which allows you to accomplish twice as much in a shorter period of time. And if you have able-bodied adult children, the number of available team members is multiplied.

3. Becoming financially free requires the right mind-set, a lot of effort, and complete dedication. This mind-set is important for a number of reasons and will be a large part of today's topic.

Have you heard the quote: "If the grass is greener on the other side, that's because your neighbor has a higher water bill"? The first thing you must do to create a financially free marriage and household—resulting in fewer arguments—is this: *Do not compare yourself, what you have, or how you live to other people, what they have, or how they live.*

STEP ONE: DO NOT COMPARE YOURSELVES TO OTHERS

Be content with what you have at this moment. You have more years to live and more material things to gain (if you choose), but in this moment, on this day, at this exact time, what you have is what you have. Learning to be content is the first step toward becoming financially free in your marriage.

Hands down, this will probably be the most difficult step you'll take throughout this process, because you will need to stop comparing. The reason this is so tough is that, for most of us, comparing ourselves to other people comes naturally. Many of us don't even realize we're doing it.

Let me ask you a question. If you and your spouse were the only two people living on earth, would you care about the house you're living in, and for that matter, would you even notice the difference between living in a house that's "owned" versus renting a home or apartment?

This may seem like a silly question, but pondering it will help you make this important first step: If you and your spouse were the only two people alive on this earth, would you be happy to watch television shows on whatever TV you owned, or would you "need" to have a sixty-inch flatscreen hanging on your wall? Would you "need" a newer car, or would the one you have work just fine because it continues to get you from point A to point B and back home again?

I remember that when Keith and I first read *The Total Money Makeover* by Dave Ramsey, we began telling everyone about it. Our brother-in-law, Tray, read the book and began working on becoming debt-free as well. One of the first people he talked to after reading it was contemplating a new car purchase and wanted to know his opinion on which car to get. He told her, "Before you consider buying a new car, I only have one request. Read *The Total Money Makeover* first."

Needless to say, she read the book and later told him, "I'm going to keep driving this car until the wheels fall off!" Several years later, she was still driving her little white Toyota with dents and dings everywhere, because she had freed herself of the "need" to buy a new car. She realized that the one she owned got her from point A to point B successfully every day, and if she wasn't comparing her car to anyone else's, it was more than enough.

Although the Great Recession, as it's been labeled, officially began in December 2007, most of us didn't feel its effects until after September 2008. Based on economists' definition of the word *recession*, the Great Recession ended in the United States around June or July 2009. Yet five years later, most Americans have felt little relief. Since this is most likely the reality in your household, I'd like to share what I've learned over the years about money and finances and how we determined to create a financially free marriage in the middle of the greatest recession since the Great Depression.

During breakfast not too long ago, I asked Keith, "If two of our married friends came to us and were having extremely difficult times financially, and those money woes were spilling into their marriage, what would you recommend their first steps be to turn it around?"

I posed this question to him for a number of reasons: (1) he's one of the wisest people I know; (2) he's read nearly every best-selling personal finance book on the market; (3) we navigated through the economic downturn together and have managed to remain relatively secure due to the plan we put in place; and (4) I wanted to make sure we were on the same page regarding the steps I will be sharing with you during the final week of this challenge.

As I suspected, we had the exact same thought as to the first three steps a couple must take to get their finances and relationship back on track. And the first two involve mind-set.

You need to change your mind-set to free yourself from being concerned about what other people have relative to what you have and to truly believe that what you have at this moment is enough. Only then will you be able to put a plan in place that can work.

Learning to stop comparing yourself to other people is one of the most difficult paradigm shifts to achieve because it is so contrary to what we have always done. Even those of us who don't think we compare ourselves to others will be surprised to learn we do.

Rick Warren wrote the runaway bestseller *The Purpose Driven Life*, selling tens of millions of copies, and he wears a watch from Walmart that cost seventeen dollars. I like to use him as an example because few people exemplify this principle of living below your means as well as he does, although Warren Buffett may have him beat in the frugality department. I considered the watches Keith and I wear and thought, *Wow. Our watches and Rick Warren's watch tell the exact same time and perform the exact same function, and yet ours cost a hundred times more.* What is the reason Keith and I chose the watches we chose? If I were to say we did it for ourselves, I'd be dishonest. I didn't know that when we purchased the watches, but I know it now.

Admitting to ourselves that much of what we do is for the consideration of other people frees us up to stop making that mistake. It's tough, I know. This is a struggle most of us have, and God bless the people who don't. I know very few.

Once you're able to answer the questions about your "needs" honestly to yourself—"If you and your spouse were the only two people alive on this earth, would you need or want all that you have or desire?"—you and your spouse can begin working on the next step.

Step Two: Simplify Your Image

No doubt, you've heard the advice in step one before, and I know it may sound too simple and you might have been looking for something more profound. But what I've found is that what is complicated and confounding is usually not what works. It is simplicity that matters most, and if you want to keep or get your marriage on track in the midst of tough financial times, not only is step one necessary, but you may find that it is the one thing that can bring immediate relief.

After Keith and I prayed for wisdom in navigating our way through the global recession so we'd grow stronger during those uncertain times, eight principles were revealed to us. The eight steps we will discuss next. But as is usually the case with all things worth having, it came at a cost.

We would have to learn to sacrifice a lot of the things we'd grown accustomed to, like traveling all over the world on twice-annual vacations. We'd have to stop going out to fancy dinners several times a week. We'd need to stop purchasing things on a whim—for both ourselves and other people. We'd need to make a lot of adjustments to our budget, and in order to do that we'd have to do one extremely difficult thing. We'd need to simplify our image and not concern ourselves with what others think.

By most standards, Keith and I are considered successful businesspeople. In the past, that made us feel entitled to certain purchases because we felt that we had worked hard and earned them. But once we became determined to pay off all our debt, we had to toss that mentality out of the window.

We remained laser-beam focused, and the plan we put in place worked faster than we thought it would, providing the opportunity for me to leave my job as a hotel general manager to focus on our real estate investments and other business-related opportunities. In the midst of the worst recession of our lifetime, I was able to quit my job and launch a company we'd kept on the back burner for five years.

However, I don't want you to think this came easily. Keith and I followed a strict financial plan as prescribed in *The Total Money Makeover* and got our mind-set straight and in one accord as husband and wife. We sacrificed a lot. But one thing we did not subtract from our budget is the very thing most people who are going through financial challenges don't realize they need to add. That brings us to step three, which we'll discuss tomorrow.

—— *Day Twenty-Three Challenge Questions* ——

1. If you and your spouse were the only two people living on earth, would you care about what kind of house, car, or TV you have? Be honest: How many of your purchases stem from a desire to please other people? Write down an example of something you've bought (electronics, brand-name clothes or accessories, etc.) because "everyone else has one" or you wanted to impress others. In what ways has this outlook on your spending habits affected your current financial situation?

2. What adjustments do you and your spouse need to make in order to reduce your spending and simplify your image? Look at your monthly budget and discuss with your spouse: What extra expenses could the two of you give up for a time in order to pay down debt and build up savings? Be specific.

3. "Learning to be content is the first step toward becoming financially free in your marriage." Whether you are currently in debt or simply planning for the future, how would your financial situation improve if you changed your mind-set to stop comparing yourselves to others and to start simplifying your image?

FOLLOW THE 10/90 RULE

YOU HAVE PROBABLY HEARD AT SOME POINT IN YOUR LIFE ABOUT the 80/10/10 rule. I grew up understanding this principle and was forced to abide by it in my parents' home. I say "forced" because what kid wants to give up 20 percent of his or her allowance each week? But in our household ignoring this rule was not an option.

If you've never heard of the 80/10/10 rule, it's quite basic: 10 percent of all your income is set aside for a tithe (giving), 10 percent is set aside as savings, and the other 80 percent is spent as you deem best. This is a formula you will hear most financial experts talk about, and it is one Keith and I highly recommend and now follow. I discovered long before I met Keith that although the 80/10/10 rule is a good goal, there is a different percentage breakdown that is required at a minimum to achieve great success.

STEP THREE: THE 10/90 RULE IS A REQUIREMENT

There are six remaining steps to creating a financially free marriage, household, and overall life. In my opinion, this step, number three, is the most important, and if it is the only step you follow, I believe you will see a change in your life. You may not become debt-free, but if this step is done with the right motive, your financial situation will begin to improve. And here it is (drumroll, please): *the first 10 percent of your income does not belong to you.* Forget about it. It doesn't exist. It comes in and it immediately goes out. It never has time to settle into your bank account; no interest ever grows on it. You are solely a funnel. It goes in and it goes out. Period.

There have been disputes about tithing as long as there have been arguments about varying theologies. Most people find it difficult to "give up" what they believe they own. But if you speak with ten wealthy individuals and ask if they donate at least 10 percent of their income, you will likely get the same answer: *yes!* They may disagree on whether the tithe needs to be given to the church or to a charity, but they will agree that the tithe, which literally means one-tenth, is the minimum amount of income that should be given away.

You don't believe me? Go to the top of *Forbes'* Richest People in America list and work your way down. Better yet, look in the top personal finance books of all time. All of them. For example, in *Rich Dad Poor Dad*, one of the best-selling personal finance books of all time, author Robert Kiyosaki says regarding tithing, "If I could leave one single idea with you, it is that idea." He wrote an entire book on what his "rich dad" taught him that "poor dads" tend not to teach their children, and tithing was the most important lesson. "My rich dad . . . believed firmly in tithing. 'If you want something, you first need to give,' he would always say. When he was short on money, he simply gave money to his church or to his favorite charity."[1]

Kiyosaki goes on to repeat something his rich dad would always say: "Poor people are more greedy than rich people."[2] He also noted that his educated "poor dad" gave a lot of his time and knowledge but almost never gave away money. What Kiyosaki explained in his book has been backed up by the wealthiest for much longer than you and I have been alive.

Just last week, as Keith was cleaning out some old boxes, he came across a copy of *Fortune* magazine dated April 1, 2002. On the cover, there is a picture of Oprah Winfrey with these words written in large letters across her face: "Oprah Inc!" On the bottom right-hand side of the cover, "Her $1 billion empire. Her no-numbers management style. And why she'll *never* give another business interview." And if my memory serves me correctly, I believe she's remained true to her word on that. But this first (and possibly only) business article was packed to the brim with great wisdom. And nestled among those words of wisdom were these: "Oprah . . . has donated at least 10% of her annual income to charity, most of it anonymously, throughout her adult life."[3]

When I saw those words, it made me smile because I knew I'd be sharing this advice with you. I am no financial guru and have no desire to be, but I can share my personal experience with you as well as other stories I've come across throughout my lifetime. Without exception, every person I've ever spoken with who has had ongoing financial challenges has not followed the 10/90 rule consistently. And without exception, every person who has decided to follow this rule consistently—especially when in the midst of a financial crisis—has seen his or her financial situation improve dramatically.

THE PRIORITY OF TITHING

When Keith and I fell in love, we did so over the phone. We were introduced by my mom-in-love and hadn't even met each other in person before we knew we'd probably spend the rest of our lives together. When we finally met for our first date, we both knew by the end of the evening that this was the last romantic relationship we would ever have. We'd each found our soul mate, and it would be for a lifetime.

Let me share a secret with you. If Keith had told me in our first discussion about tithing that he wasn't comfortable with giving 10 percent, we would not be married today. It makes me incredibly sad to even think about my life without Keith, and I'm so happy I don't have to think about it beyond this moment and that I only have to do so now for the purpose of writing this section.

Here is the reason I would not have married Keith—in spite of my undying love for him—if we were not in one accord regarding the necessity of giving away at least a tenth of our income: I knew our household would not be fully blessed without tithing. I know that the principle of tithing works, and I have experienced it firsthand.

Somewhere around my early twenties, I began "borrowing" from the envelope I kept my tithes in each week. Keith says he thinks "borrowing" was better than not giving at all, because at least I was acknowledging the tithe did not belong to me. I think he's just being nice because he loves his wife. Here's what I know for sure. As long as I was not taking the first 10 percent of my income and giving it away, I was always in debt. No matter how much I made, I never had enough to make it to the next paycheck. Hand-to-mouth was my reality.

One day I looked at my tithe envelope where I'd recorded all the money I'd "borrowed" and I realized there was no way I could pay it back. I'd gotten in too deep. I made a commitment to God that I've never broken: "If you'll get me out of this financial mess,

I will never borrow from your tithe again. Never." This promise is the reason I would not have married Keith if he hadn't been committed to tithing.

It took about six months for me to get out of the financial mess I'd made, but I tithed from the moment I said that prayer. From that day forward, the tithe has passed through my hands. It does not stop even for a moment. As soon as the money comes in, a check goes out, like a game of hot potato. But I don't just believe in the principle of tithing because the wealthy do it and because it is something I believe kept me from living hand-to-mouth for most of my adult life. I believe it because I've also seen it work in the life of *every* person I know who has committed to doing it.

A PREREQUISITE TO FINANCIAL FREEDOM

Throughout the years, I've had the pleasure of helping people get their personal finances in order. I never made a business of it; I simply enjoy doing it. But there has always been one condition for my agreement to help: the person I'm helping must tithe. I don't want to waste my time giving advice or spend my resources trying to help people organize their debt and spending habits if they're not willing to give away 10 percent.

About fifteen years ago, a family member came to me because she and her husband were experiencing financial challenges. It was not a rare occurrence for their lights, gas, or water to be turned off. The situation was taking a toll on their relationship and their life.

I made them a deal. I would act as their business manager. We would set up a household bank account where each of their paychecks would be deposited. I would then give each of them an allowance to cover all their needs and a reasonable number of their wants each month. (I'll say more about "needs versus wants" in the next chapter.) I would pay all their bills from their household account and supply them with a monthly statement so they'd know exactly how much they had and how much they were saving.

I agreed to do all this under one condition and one condition only: they would have to begin tithing—immediately. They could not argue with me about it. They could never question it. Ten percent of their income would be given away the moment their paychecks were deposited.

What happened over the next year will probably not be a surprise to you. Within a few months my family members saw their financial situation begin to stabilize. They were offered several freelance jobs, which allowed even more money to begin coming in to pay off their debt.

Within a year they were nearly debt-free, and by the next year they were putting a down payment on a four-bedroom home in a beautiful California neighborhood. It may surprise you to learn that the home was offered to them at nearly half its actual value. They started off with equity in their home, and a lot of it.

Stories like this are not rare. This has happened to all the people I know who have begun tithing and have committed to becoming better stewards of the other 90 percent of their income. When a couple comes to me with financial challenges, I ask the following two questions:

1. Are you tithing?
2. What are you doing with the other 90 percent?

Even though I plan to ask two questions, I usually only ask one. I rarely get to the second question, because for the people

I've met who are struggling financially, the first answer is almost always no. No, they're not tithing. And thus I know where to advise them to begin. In the one instance in which a couple responded that they'd been tithing, Keith and I were both stumped. We'd never run into an instance in which a couple having continuous financial challenges were also tithers. We remained baffled for a few months until we learned the *whole* story. The couple was tithing "when they could." Sometimes they would, and sometimes they wouldn't.

Overcome Your Objections to Tithing

I've *never* known one couple or one individual who continued to struggle after they've applied the 10/90 rule consistently. Determine to begin giving 10 percent today, because people who learn to live on less than 90 percent will always have more than people who live on 100 percent.

—— *Day Twenty-Four Challenge Questions* ——

1. "The first 10 percent of your income does not belong to you. Forget about it. . . . It goes in and it goes out. Period." What is your honest reaction to that statement? Do you believe that following the 10/90 rule will have a positive impact on your finances? Consider some advantages of a generous lifetyle—what positive effects would giving a tithe of your income have on you, your marriage, your family, and your community?

2. If you have been tithing regularly, what effects have you experienced in your finances? If you have doubts about

following the 10/90 rule, how do you respond to the following statement? "Without exception, every person who has decided to follow this rule consistently—especially when in the midst of a financial crisis—has seen his or her financial situation improve dramatically."

3. If you are not currently tithing to a church or charity, what is preventing you from following the 10/90 rule in your finances? Write down some of your objections to giving away a tithe of your income, such as "don't have enough money," "the pastor doesn't need it," etc. How did the lessons you learned in today's reading help you overcome any possible objections?

MORE MONEY, LESS STUFF

DO YOU REMEMBER WHEN YOU WERE YOUNG AND COULDN'T wait until the end of the week for your allowance? I certainly do. I'd wash my dad's car, pull weeds from the backyard, clean the grout between the kitchen tiles with a toothbrush, and clean the glass around the house with Windex and newspaper. By the end of the week, I was ready for that allowance!

Are you ready for a radical idea for married adults? Well, it's coming at you right now.

STEP FOUR: ALLOWANCE ISN'T JUST FOR KIDS

Keith and I began giving ourselves an allowance as one of our first steps to financial freedom. We began doing this because we realized that, more often than not, a monthly budget is just a number on a piece of paper. It is a goal, like a New Year's resolution. But the number of people with credit cards who manage to stick to their budget is about the same as the number of people who stick to their annual resolutions.

I don't remember exactly where or from whom we learned about giving ourselves an allowance, but continuing to do so throughout all these years has helped us stay on track financially. In the subsequent article to the *Money* survey I discussed earlier, the experts suggest allowing for money autonomy to create greater harmony in your marriage: "With your spouse, agree on a monthly amount that you'll each put into separate accounts, to be used at your discretion." Pepper Schwartz, sociologist and coauthor of *The Surprising Secrets of Happy Couples*, adds to that point: "Research has found that the happiest couples have a joint account for the essentials and then some discretionary money."[1]

Here's how it works in our home. All our income goes into a joint household checking account, and each month we both get an agreed-upon "allowance." That money is the maximum we commit to spend that month on our personal needs, and we stick to it. We decide in advance who will pay for what out of his or her allowance. For instance, groceries might come out of my allowance while date nights might come out of Keith's. We determined our allowances based on needs and a few wants. And by needs, I mean necessities.

To determine my needs, I tracked my expenses for a month or two by obtaining receipts for every single purchase I made and making every purchase in cash. I even recorded something as small as a pack of gum. If I spent money, I tracked it. At the end of the month, I was able to ascertain which expenses were "needs" and which were "wants."

The process of determining needs versus wants can become complicated if we allow it to. But really it should be simple. For example, cable is a "want," while Internet, depending on what you do for a living, may be a "need." Coffee may be important to you as a pick-me-up if that's what your body is accustomed to in the morning. But a $4 cup of coffee or a Frappuccino from Starbucks definitely falls under the "want" category.

For women, identifying the difference between needs and wants can get pretty tricky when it comes to personal beautification. Going to a salon to get your hair done or to get a manicure and pedicure is a "want." Looking presentable for work and for everyday life is important, but there are many ways to get there. I can count on one hand the number of manicures and pedicures I got at a salon during the first two years we were working our debt-free financial plan. And my hairdresser, who at one point saw me every week, saw me only bimonthly for a trim during the years we were working on setting ourselves financially free.

As long as there are grass and concrete outside to run or walk on and videos you can buy or rent to exercise with at home, gym memberships are a "want." I went from spending $150 per month to exercise at an upscale gym to $0 per month to run a few miles and practice yoga using a DVD. And you know what? I got into the best shape of my life.

Buying a new shirt because the one you have is "so last season" is definitely a "want." Purchasing another pair of shoes when you already have ten pairs is also a "want," no matter how "necessary" it is. Even purchases in the grocery store need to be divided between "needs" and "wants." I'm not saying life should be boring and you shouldn't have a lot of your "wants"; the advisability of such purchases just depends on where you are financially.

After Keith and I paid off all our debt (excluding mortgages), we returned to slightly more liberal spending habits for a short period of time. But once we became actively engaged in paying off our mortgages, we once again reined in our spending quite a

THE ARGUMENT-FREE MARRIAGE

bit and returned to limiting ourselves mainly to our "needs" while sprinkling in a few "wants" here and there.

After you've determined not to participate in any future recession and to begin dumping any financial debt you might be carrying, embracing radical ideas may be necessary. When Keith and I started making some of our more drastic changes to curb our spending habits and told my brother-in-law about it, he sent a text that read, "You've got some NURV!" That acronym, borrowed from a movie, is exactly what we're discssing in the final week of this challenge: Never Underestimate Radical Vision.

Even daring to talk about becoming debt-free while still in the midst of a slow economic recovery takes a lot of NURV. And creating a financial plan that keeps you on track should be just as radical. And a weekly, biweekly, or monthly allowance may just do the trick.

Everyone's different, but I'll share with you my plan. Each month I deposit my allowance amount into a personal checking account. And Keith does the same. I then withdraw one-fifth of the total amount in cash. This is what I give myself for the upcoming week.

What's great about keeping an allowance in a separate account is that there is no extra money to spend. Once it's gone, it's gone, so this system forces you to spend wisely throughout each week and throughout the month. The reason I withdraw one-fifth each week instead of one-fourth is because I want to keep a little extra in the account just in case I come across a "want" I *really, really* want.

I realize this system may be a little too radical for some. Many people like having more flexibility. And I recognize that one size does not fit all. But I can tell you that it's worth a try. Track your receipts this month, even for bubble gum, and tally them up at the end of the month. Then separate the purchase receipts into two piles. The first pile should be for items you purchased that were needed. Use the total from this pile as a basis for determining your monthly allowance.

Test this system for a few months and see how much you save. Really, what do you have to lose? If you don't like it, go back to what you were doing before. My desire is to see you debt-free and not arguing with your spouse over finances.

Step Five: Let Stuff Go

Have you ever tried catching a monkey? Probably not, if you live in the United States, but maybe you've heard of one method. In Africa, as the story goes, people cut a coconut in half, hollow it out, put a ripe orange in the middle, and then seal the coconut back together, leaving only a hole small enough for a monkey to get its hand through. They then use rope to secure the coconut to a tree. Then they wait.

Soon enough, an unsuspecting monkey swings by, smells the orange, and sticks its thin hand into the coconut. It grabs the treat and then attempts to pull its hand out. Unfortunately for the monkey, the hole is only large enough for it to get its hand in or out if its hand is empty. With its fist clenched around the orange, the monkey is not able to remove its hand. The monkey continues to try until a net is thrown over it and it is caught.

During the entire time the monkey is trying to remove its hand from the coconut, it never dawns on it to simply let go. And thus the greedy monkey leads us to our fifth step in this eight-step process. For some people, the first four steps in this plan for a financially free marriage are enough. But for others, the solution is not as simple as adopting a radical vision for emerging from the pits of debt or merely becoming determined to free their family from the bondage of this self-imposed slavery. If this is the case for you, then steps one through four will only get you halfway there. You need more. Steps five and six are specifically for you.

Could letting go of certain material possessions you're holding on to bring you greater peace? In the past year or so, we've recommended to more people than I can remember that they short-sale their home. No, it's not the ideal solution, but if a home is causing such a financial burden that it's become a tremendous weight on your family, walk away. A deed in lieu of foreclosure, a short sale, it doesn't matter. Just figure out the most responsible way to let it go.

Do you know of people who have so much stuff that they pay for storage space? Are you one of those people? If so, this is where you can start. Clearly, the things in storage are not items you're using every day. They'd probably fall under the category of excess. Yes, they might be things you plan to use at a later date, but we're talking about freeing your family from debt.

Pull together all the stuff you don't need; gather anything in storage that can be replaced at a later date when your family is in a better financial position. And have a big ol' garage sale. Yep, I said it. Sell that stuff! Go online and sell it on eBay, Craigslist, and anywhere else you can unload your family extras. Start purging yourself of things you no longer need. Free up as much cash as possible so you can begin paying off your debt. The faster you can pay off the principal of something you've previously put on credit, the sooner you can stop wasting precious dollars on interest.

I don't think it's necessary for me to give you a step-by-step plan on letting stuff go. You know how to do it. You just have to make up your mind to do it. It might be tough at first, but look at it a different way. Picture all the extra stuff you have as a weight on your shoulders. Then as you sell one item and then another and then another, that weight continues to get lighter and lighter.

Here's the bottom line for step five: don't be a monkey. Debt and material possessions are only a trap if you refuse to unclench your fist. But once you determine to start letting stuff go, you'll begin to taste the freedom your heart desires.

—— *Day Twenty-Five Challenge Questions* ——

1. Do you and your spouse currently stay on track financially with an allowance? If so, discuss how this practice has helped your financial situation. If not, discuss how having a joint bank account and budgeting an allowance (the maximum each of you commits to spend each month) could assist you on your journey to financial freedom.

2. Determine your household's monthly "needs" versus "wants." First, make a list of your actual necessities for living —mortgage or rent, groceries, utilities, etc. Then make a separate list of your "wants"—eating meals at restaurants, manicures/pedicures, leisure activities, etc. If you have difficulty ascertaining "needs" versus "wants," consider spending only cash for one month and tracking all your expenses. Talk through both lists with your spouse and then agree on an amount each spouse will be allotted per month as "allowance." Designate which expenses will be covered by which spouse.

3. Are there any material possessions you're holding on to that would bring you greater peace if you let them go? Pull

together all the stuff you don't need and have a garage sale (or sell items online). Designate all proceeds from the sale toward paying down debt. Write on your calendar the date of your garage sale or deadline to sell online and work toward the goal of simplifying your stuff.

REDEFINE THE AMERICAN DREAM

SEVERAL YEARS AGO I BEGAN TO RECONSIDER THE IMPLICATIONS of the American Dream. The more I listened to people talk about it, the more I became convinced that the American Dream, as it's currently described, is really just the American (in) Debt. I began to think about how the American Dream was first described and was intrigued by its transformation over the past century into a vision that now includes a house with a white picket fence and a hefty thirty-year mortgage.

Recently I watched the film *A Raisin in the Sun* for the first time. I'd never had the opportunity to see the critically acclaimed play, so the on-screen production was the next best thing. One of the main plots involves an African American family in the mid-1900s torn apart by a ten-thousand-dollar life insurance policy from the deceased husband of the matriarch. Her only son spends most of the movie lobbying to take the check the moment it arrives and invest it in their future. By "future," I mean he wants to invest it in a scheme that seems promising. Infighting ensues among family members over their differences in opinion regarding how the matriarch of the family should spend the money once the postman delivers the check.

By the end of the movie, the matriarch has relented and hesitantly gives her son sixty-five hundred dollars, of which three thousand is supposed be put in a bank for his sister's college education. Unfortunately, he "invests" the three thousand dollars, and within days he learns that one of his new business partners is a con artist and has skipped town with the money. In spite of all that, the family somehow finds solace in the fact that the first thirty-five hundred dollars was used as a down payment on a home they all move into in the final scenes of the movie.

Once the credits began to roll, I turned to Keith and said, "That was depressing." Keith was surprised, because the movie is an American classic and presumably most viewers don't react this way to its "happy" ending. After all, the film contains a strong message about the housing discrimination that occurred prior to the Fair Housing Act of 1968. And at the end the family is all hugs and laughter as they begin moving into their new home. But all I could think about was that they were now in debt.

Yes, their apartment wasn't ideal, but why not just get a slightly nicer apartment? Instead, they move into a home for which they cannot afford the monthly payments. The daughter-in-law exclaims she'll work twenty hours a day, if she has to, in order to help pay the mortgage. The matriarch of the family, who retired at the beginning of the movie, will now need to return to work to also help pay the mortgage.

I told Keith, "This isn't a happy ending. They're all in debt!" These words renewed my thought that the American Dream has somewhere along the years lost its meaning and that now is the time for us to return to the basics. Although step six is titled "Redefine the American Dream," it could as easily be titled, "Return to the *Original* American Dream." That just wasn't as catchy.

Step Six: Redefine the American Dream

What do you think about when you hear the term *American Dream*? If a house with a white picket fence enters your mind, or home ownership at all for that matter, then you and I are in the same boat: completely brainwashed.

I am a self-proclaimed research junkie, so recently I began looking at the American Dream and was reminded of the enormous gift I was given simply by the latitude and longitude in which I was born.

Historian James Truslow Adams, who popularized the phrase " the American Dream" in his 1931 book *Epic of America,* said, "Life should be better and richer and fuller for everyone, with opportunity for each according to ability or achievement,"[1] regardless of social class or circumstances of birth. The idea of the American Dream is rooted in the United States Declaration of Independence, which proclaims that "all men are created equal" and that we are all "endowed by [our] Creator with certain inalienable Rights," including "Life, Liberty and the pursuit of Happiness."

Truslow Adams also observed, "The American dream, that has lured tens of millions of all nations to our shores in the past century has . . . been a dream of being able to grow to fullest development as man and woman, unhampered by the barriers which had slowly been erected in the older civilizations, unrepressed by social orders which had developed for the benefit of classes rather than for the simple human being of any and every class."[2]

During the past few years, I've heard so many people say, "The American Dream is over. It's been lost forever." But if the American Dream is about life, liberty, and the pursuit of happiness, then why would that change because the economy shifts downward? If freedom of expression, religion, and speech, and all the other inalienable rights of human beings, as defined by our Declaration of Independence, are still fully intact, what is it we've actually lost?

The answer is simple: in 2009, most Americans figured out they weren't actually free. It was just a false perception. Here's a large part of what happens in a recession: (1) money gets tight, and banks stop extending loans and credit lines; (2) credit limits are drastically reduced; (3) home equity lines of credit are immediately frozen or reduced; and (4) the housing market plummets.

When you examine the items in the preceding list, do you see a trend? The items listed all show that everyone is living or functioning on borrowed dollars. Businesses requiring lines of credit to continue operating suddenly find themselves needing to function on their actual income. Consumers who have been scraping by month to month on their credit cards suddenly find that the well has dried up and they, too, must begin living within their means.

Did you know that most thirty-year fixed home loans are set up so that during the first fifteen years you're solely paying interest? No, really. When people finish paying off their thirty-year loans, in most instances, their homes have cost them more than double the purchase price. So for a $350,000 home, the buyer ends up paying more than $700,000. This is one of the reasons Robert Kiyosaki, in his book *Rich Dad Poor Dad*, vigorously challenges the argument that a home is an asset if there is a mortgage attached. Something similar happens when you "buy" a car on credit.

June 3, 2014, the *Wall Street Journal* announced the results of a new survey, commissioned by the nonprofit John D. and Catherine T. MacArthur Foundation and carried out by Hart Research Associates. In the article, "Half of Americans Can't Afford Their House," Stuart Gabriel, the director of UCLA's Richard S. Ziman Center for Real Estate, is quoted as saying, "From a policy perspective, we overshot in prescribing home-ownership too often and to those who would have benefited more from other housing solutions." The article then gives a sobering statistic: "In the years after the recession of 2008, more than 7.5 million homeowners lost their home to foreclosure or short sale and about 9 million more homeowners are still underwater and owe more than their property is worth."[3]

The article goes on to quote real estate data expert Daren Blomquist: "If one looks at the last seven years as a predictor of housing market behavior in the future, it certainly should give one pause about whether buying a home is a good investment or not."[4]

Then, as is almost always the case when discussing a survey on the housing market, talk of the American Dream is introduced: "Some people also appear to be cooling on one facet of the American dream. . . . Although 70 percent of renters aspire to own a home, some 58 percent believe that 'renters can be just as successful as owners at achieving the American dream.'"[5]

That's good news. I'm not suggesting that purchasing a home is a bad idea or that holding a mortgage is a mistake. If that's the case, Keith and I are the holders of quite a few "mistakes." It's a question of affordability and of whether keeping a mortgage while pulling yourself out of debt is wise. Only you can answer that question for your family.

Maybe what is keeping you in debt is not a home but rather something seemingly smaller: credit. When you put a $2,500 big-screen television on your credit card, do you know how much that television is really costing you? Let's just say that if you put it on a credit card with an interest rate of 18 percent and make the minimum payments every month, it will take you roughly twenty-eight years to pay off that television. For your $2,500 purchase, you will end up paying a total of $8,397 by the time it's all said and done, and $5,897 of that will be in interest payments.

Most of us have been brainwashed into using credit as a regular part of our lives. Psychologists have worked with corporations and advertising firms for decades to help them understand the best way to tap into the emotions of individuals to get them to forget reason and to satisfy their "wants" immediately. We've been taught to require instant gratification.

How do we hop off this hamster wheel? The first five steps in this plan to create a financially free household are a good start. And this sixth step requires learning to live below your means. You need to reject the version of the American Dream that involves living as a slave to the lender. Then you can create an American Dream for your family or just return to the original dream that involved life, liberty, the pursuit of happiness—and freedom.

Taking your life back from creditors can be tough, depending on how long you've been living a "charged up" lifestyle. It's absolutely possible, and it can begin today. But it involves having the right mind-set. You need to be more concerned about your marital happiness and freedom than about your image or what others might say or think about you.

The best way not to participate in a recession is to take away the ability of others to control any portion of your life. Think about it this way. Do you think that people who were living below their means when the recession began, and weren't overextending themselves with credit cards or any other form of credit, have been debilitated by the recession? They may have been affected, which would be normal for anyone living in an ailing society, but has the recession altered their entire lives? Has it turned their lives upside down?

Begin tightening your belt today, because if history is a reliable indicator, within a few years of this economic turnaround, we'll be headed for another recession. The difference is that this time you and your family will not be a part of it.

——— *Day Twenty-Six Challenge Questions* ———

1. What comes to your mind when you hear someone discuss the American Dream? What kinds of things do most people think they need to possess in order to achieve the American Dream? How has the American Dream changed over the years from its original version? In what ways has this shift of perspective affected your expectations of the possessions you think you need or deserve?

2. Are you currently relying on credit cards for your monthly expenses? If so, pull out your most recent credit card statements and add up how much you spent the last month on interest alone. How much money could you save by avoiding those interest payments? Commit today to start paying off your credit card debt. For assistance in making an action plan to pay off your credit cards, read "How to Get Out of Debt" on www.DaveRamsey.com.

3. Write out a new definition of the American Dream.

Discuss with your spouse specific ways you can begin to live below your means. Decide together that you will reject the version of the American Dream that involves living as a slave to the lender and instead begin working toward financial freedom.

ROME WASN'T BUILT IN A DAY

WHEN I FIRST BEGAN WRITING ABOUT FINANCES, I THOUGHT it would be no longer than a few pages. I'd share a few thoughts and hope you'd glean enough from them to begin on the path toward financial freedom. Quite frankly, I thought I was just going to share with you that my number one piece of financial advice was to invest in Dave Ramsey's *The Total Money Makeover*, and then I'd be done with it.

Now, six days and six steps later, we are finally nearing the end. For some of you, the first six steps in this plan for a financially free marriage are all you'll need to get on the right track. But for those who find yourselves buried in debt, figuring out creative ways to bring more income into the family may be required.

STEP SEVEN: LOOK FOR NEW
INCOME OPPORTUNITIES

When times are tough, money is tight, and the bills are mounting, obtaining another job may be necessary. A secondary job is never ideal, and it's rarely enjoyable, but it may be needed. Now is the time to put your heads together and figure out how you can bring more money into your household. That may mean working one job from 7:00 a.m. to 3:00 p.m. and another from 4:00 p.m. to 10:00 p.m. Working twelve-hour days, six days a week is exhausting. I understand. My husband understands. We've both done it multiple times throughout our careers. Seventy-plus hours of work each week is definitely no laughing matter, but it may be necessary for the time being to create more income for your family. And it should be temporary.

Set a goal of getting out of debt. Lay out all your bills and begin calculating the length of time it will take you to pay them all off. There are tons of websites that can show you effective ways to do this. After you've determined how long it will take you to pay them off at your current household income, calculate how much time you can shave off by bringing in more money. The sooner you can get it done, the sooner you can experience the financial freedom you long to have.

Many people reading this book may be stay-at-home moms or dads. If that's the case, you already know you have one of the most exhausting and underappreciated jobs in the world. But, and this may surprise you, it is also one that can potentially give you the flexibility to add another source of revenue to the family's bottom line.

There are plenty of creative ways to make money, and if you look online for testimonials, you'll run out of time before you run out of success stories. But one of my favorite strategies is making your services available through sites like Elance and oDesk and expanding your job opportunities from the United States or wherever you are located to the worldwide job market.

When I mention Elance or oDesk to people, it's rare for me

to come across someone who knows what I'm talking about. But these companies have been a conduit for pairing work with qualified workers for some time now, and contractors (people like you) have earned more than $700 million on the Elance and oDesk platforms. More than six million employers hire freelancers using these two services, which recently merged to form one company, although the two sites continue to operate separately. Personally, I prefer Elance. In the past I've hired contractors from California, Tennessee, Florida, Canada, Costa Rica, India, Argentina, and the Philippines, and there are thousands of small businesses just like mine that look for talented workers through sites like Elance.

Many people think these sites are solely for workers from other countries who work for less than $5 per hour. That is absolutely not true. When I hire contractors for various projects, I pay no less than the US minimum wage for work on my websites, social media, content management, IT support—no matter where a worker is located—and the average wage I currently pay my contractors is $18 per hour. If you live in the United States, there's a good chance you have a laptop or desktop computer in your home. If you have a computer, you can learn the skills needed to earn extra income online. There is a bustling online marketplace where businesses like mine look for people like you who are hardworking, dedicated, and skilled.

I bet many of you would be shocked to find out that you can learn to build websites at the highest level for free and become a programmer. And people around the world do it every day. There is an organization called the World Wide Web Consortium (W3C), which was founded by the inventor of the World Wide Web, Tim Berners-Lee. That's right, every time you enter "www" followed by a period and then a word, remember that the "www" was invented by one person. And Berners-Lee has always maintained that the web should be open and everyone should be able to learn how to operate, create, and build on it—for free. You can learn everything you'll ever need to know about programming by going to w3schools.com.

Maybe you have no desire to learn how to write code for websites. There's still plenty you can do. If you like talking on the phone, make yourself available as a customer service rep. Did you know that when you call companies like JetBlue, you're actually speaking to a reservation agent working from home? Yes, every one of their eight hundred–plus reservation agents is taking your call from his or her own home. If you type fast and your work is accurate, offer data entry services. Do you enjoy research as much as I do? Become a research specialist. And all this can be done on sites like Elance, oDesk, Guru, and others.

Because I've hired so many workers through these sites, these services are what I think of immediately when people tell me they're willing to work more to get out of debt but just need to find a job. If you've been looking and can't find a second job, create one. Technology isn't the only way. Most virtual assistants service multiple clients at a time, billing each from $20 to $50 per hour. Figure out which of your skills can be used from home, and then pursue jobs requiring that skill set. You may have to get creative, but there is something out there if you're willing to take the time to find it. Have a family meeting and ask yourselves, what can we do together to bring more income into our home?

After you've figured out a way to bring more income into your household, the important thing to remember is that the purpose of this additional income is to pay off debt you've already incurred. Don't go spending it; that defeats the purpose. Pretend this money doesn't even exist; it comes in, you apply the 10/90 principle to it, and you keep it moving. Keep your mind squarely focused on creating a financially free marriage and household, and it will happen. It may take some time, but stay the course.

STEP EIGHT: BE PATIENT AND DON'T LOSE HEART

Rome wasn't built in a day, and your financial solution won't be either. Be patient and diligent as you begin this road to financial freedom. Your reward will far outweigh your sacrifice. Finances are a tricky topic because many people would simply prefer to ignore financial difficulties until they can no longer be ignored. I once had a business partner who would leave his bills unopened. There was something about not opening the bills that allowed him to pretend they weren't there. It's like one of my favorite episodes of *I Love Lucy,* in which Lucy is put in charge of paying the bills. She finds them all overwhelming and gets behind in her payments, so she comes up with a simple solution. She puts all the bills on a lazy Susan and spins it as fast as she can. Whichever bills remain on the "spinning thing" are the ones she will pay.

It's classic Lucy and certainly makes for a hilarious episode. But unfortunately, that's how a lot of us handle debt. We pretend it is not there until we can no longer ignore it. By that time, there's a mounting pile of bills that need to be paid. And even if we make all the minimum payments, it seems never to decrease. That's one of the reasons people get discouraged when they begin a mission to pay off their debt.

I won't attempt to give you a step-by-step plan for paying off your debt here, because then the book would go on for another two weeks, and that would be unnecessary. As I've mentioned in nearly every chapter of this final week, for this purpose I highly recommend Dave Ramsey's *The Total Money Makeover* for you and your spouse. It will help you team up to beat your financial foe rather than turning on each other during this stressful time. And rest assured, I don't know Dave, and my endorsement of his book provides no benefit to me whatsoever. But my hope is that it will provide you with the same benefit it gave Keith and me when we followed it, making a few tweaks here and there that made sense for us.

You can also find websites online with free advice for paying off your debt and step-by-step plans to accomplish it. I suggest you Google "how to pay off debt" and then find the one that makes the most sense for you and your family. Once you've found the right plan, just begin. Beginning is 40 percent of the battle. The other 60 percent is having the patience to see it through until the end.

When Keith and I first began paying off our debt, we were extremely strict. We ate like college students on a minimal weekly budget (canned tuna and chicken, anyone?), but we could do this because we were squarely focused on paying off our debt. We remained focused the entire time.

During my morning walk a few days ago, I began thinking about something the instructor in my yoga video says right before we begin a balancing pose: "Find a focal point; it helps with balance." Anyone who does yoga knows that if you begin a balancing pose and do not have and maintain a visual focal point, you will topple right over. Alternatively, if you find a focal point and keep your eyes focused, you can remain balanced.

The same is the case with dancers. Have you ever watched children spin around in excitement several times and then start stumbling because they've lost their balance? What about you? Do you remember the last time you spun around in circles and how dizzy you got afterward? Yet a dancer can spin dozens of times, without a break, and will never get dizzy. Do you know why?

Dancers fix their gaze on a fixed point with every spin. If you videotape dancers and then watch the tape in slow motion, you will notice that their heads turn well before the rest of their bodies. They do not take their eyes off their focal point (except for a fraction of a second). This technique is called "spotting."

Most people were in debt long before they realized it. They grew so accustomed to using credit that, until the recession began, they didn't even realize they had gone so far into debt. But after you determine as a family to climb out of that financial hole, do so with all your effort and might and remain patient with the process.

There's an old saying: "By the inch it's a cinch; by the mile it's a trial." Take the steps described in the final week of this book. Determine that you're going to change your mind-set about image, recognizing that what matters most is the peace in your marriage, not what others might think about how much you have or what you just bought.

One of the things I truly believe helped Keith and me is that we told everyone close to us that we were beginning this financial journey. We let them know in advance not to expect expensive presents and to expect us to be extremely frugal when we went out with them. After seeing our excitement as we began paying off our debt, many of them decided to join us and they, too, began the journey to financial freedom. Sharing what we were doing with others also made it much easier for us to stay the course.

Determine the right plan for paying off your debt, and simply begin. And then continue. And continue some more. One of the other things Keith and I did was give ourselves a reward for every major debt we paid off. A few days away was usually the reward we chose, but maybe your reward will be going to your favorite nice restaurant, or your reward might be purchasing something you've wanted but have delayed buying for months. It can feel discouraging to work sixty to seventy hours a week and then come home and eat like a broke teenager. That's why we gave ourselves gifts with every milestone. Just do what's right for your family. What's important is that you stay the course.

You won't meet your goals overnight, but your road to financial freedom is just as much a part of the journey as the destination itself. Make the most of it as a team, and don't lose focus.

——— *Day Twenty-Seven Challenge Questions* ———

1. Set a goal of getting out of debt. Set out all your bills and calculate how long it will take you to pay them off. Once you've determined how long it will take you to pay them off at your current household income, then calculate how much time you could shave off by bringing in more money.
2. There are a ton of creative ways to earn additional income. Search websites like Elance and oDesk for job opportunities. Make a list of income possibilities you find online or through other outlets, such as home-based businesses or child care. Show this list to your spouse and discuss the viability of working a second job, for a period of time, to earn extra income that will help you achieve your financial goals.
3. Be patient and diligent as you begin this road to financial freedom. Determine the right plan for paying off your debt and simply begin. Buy Dave Ramsey's *The Total Money Makeover*, research information online, or talk to a professional financial adviser about next steps. Be sure to tell your friends and family about your decison so they can

support you on your journey toward financial freedom. And most of all, don't give up! Do what's right for your family, stay the course, and you will reap the rewards of an argument-free marriage.

MAKE THE BEST CHOICE

IF THROUGHOUT THE LAST SIX DAYS OF THIS CHALLENGE you and your spouse decided to begin your journey to financial freedom in your marriage, know that there may be times when you don't make the right decision, and that a poor decision or series of decisions could cause you to become discouraged and lose focus. Don't let it. While reprogramming ourselves to live below our means and not care about the opinions of others, Keith and I have made more mistakes than I'd like to admit. Advertisers and marketers have spent decades wooing you into thinking you "need" more to be happy and flat-out telling you that what you have is not enough. That is not easy to undo overnight.

MISTAKES ARE OKAY—EVEN WHEN IT COMES TO FINANCES

You may have started your journey toward financial freedom and then got sidetracked. It's okay. Keith and I did that too. It seems like at least once a year we have the same *aha* moment about our budget and finances and have to rein our spending back in. This is normal for anyone who didn't learn frugality from an early age. Just chalk it up to being completely normal.

My goal in sharing with you what Keith and I have discovered through the years is simply to encourage you to create the best version of your own marriage. Our marriage is no better than yours or vice versa. They are just different. I hope that something I've shared over these past seven days will have a positive impact on your marriage, especially in the area of finances and greatly reducing finances-related arguments. But more important is that you be inspired to team up with your spouse to overcome any financial stresses you may experience.

Above all else, have faith in each other and in your marriage. The two of you, no matter what comes your way, can get through it together. Just make the commitment to have no plan B, and life from here can go nowhere but up.

THE GIFT WE TAKE FOR GRANTED

Single men and women walk around hoping for the day they will find the person of their dreams. Seminars are taught all over the country to singles, helping them become content during their wait for this joyous thing called marriage. Women and men are looking for that special someone, a person who will partner with them through life. And yet those of us who are married often take that gift for granted.

You are incredibly blessed. I am unbelievably fortunate. We have found that special someone who has pledged the rest of their days to us. We should be celebrating, dancing in the streets, yelling from the rooftops that we found what so many are still hoping to find. Yet many spend an unconscionable amount of time arguing and fighting with the one they love.

When was the last time you won an argument? How did it feel? Were you exhilarated by convincing your spouse that you were right and he or she was wrong? Did your friends pat you on the back for a job well done? What did you gain? More important, what did you lose? Did you argue because you didn't want to take the time to form a more thoughtful expression of words that would accurately share how you felt? Did you want the instant gratification of an apology or an admission of guilt? What caused the argument? What was truly won in the end?

The women in the Happy Wives Club provided me with so much material for this book. Almost one thousand women sent in suggestions and advice for me to pass on to other married women. One wife wrote, "I have been married for just over thirty-three years. My husband and I don't argue, believe it or not. I think the key is to not be selfish and not worry about the small stuff. One thing I tried to instill in my kids was to stop and think about how important an issue is. I tell my kids to stop and put it on a scale of importance from 1 to 10. Yes, we do say please and thank you to one another!"

Another submitted this: "I have a good sense of humor. My husband tells everyone I married him because he makes me laugh, and that is probably true. You cannot stay angry when you are laughing! It's true. Laughter is the best medicine. And of course, never ever go to bed angry."

One of my favorite quotes from the early years of the club came from a woman married seven years. "Don't be afraid to have fun. Play and laugh as much as possible. Act silly, play games, make jokes, challenge him to a footrace back to the car, have a flower-petal fight. You shouldn't just be married; you should be best friends."

I've learned so much from these women, including these principles, which I continue to believe: We should not only love our spouses, but be best friends. Marriage wasn't meant to be so intense, so serious; it was meant to be fun and enjoyable—the partnership of a lifetime. We should be completely enamored with our spouses and everything about them.

WHAT WILL YOU CHOOSE?

The next time you think about starting an argument or responding to your spouse in a way that could escalate into an argument, think about your spouse, your best friend, and ask yourself this question: Is what I will gain worth what could be lost? If you slammed the door for the very last time, walked out of the house, and then received a call four hours later saying that your husband or wife had been in a terrible accident and passed away, would you really want that argument to be the last conversation you had with her or him? Or would you rather know that your husband or wife transitioned from this life to the next hearing the words "I love you"?

The choice is yours.

——— *Day Twenty-Eight Challenge Questions* ———

1. What is your greatest takeaway from this twenty-eight-day challenge? What can you begin implementing today to create a marriage with less arguing and more love and laughter?

2. Did you think an argument-free marriage was possible when you began this book? Do you believe it now?
3. Consider sharing this book with a married friend you believe can truly benefit from it. A world with happy and healthy marriages is a beautiful place.

ACKNOWLEDGMENTS

THANK YOU, ABBA. YOUR GRACE AND KINDNESS NEVER ceases to amaze me.

Thank you, my love, best friend, angel on earth, Keith.

My family, too large to name everyone, so I'll just stick to those around me most: Mom Wilson, Mom Scott, Pop, Tracey, Franko, Launi (and Carlos), Christy Joy (and Tray), Gabrielle, Lee, Arlene, Brett, Scott, Nancy, Jonathan, and Ellie. Thank you for loving me in spite of me.

My U.N., Zie Zie, Jocelyn, Angie, Kim, Miesa, Tyeasha, Kai. Thank you for your love, support, crazy (in a good way) ideas, and never letting me put out a book with a bad cover.

Maggie: you are a light that outshines every light.

Thank you, Dr. Gary Chapman, for honoring me with the foreword for this book. Thank you for praying about it and then acting on that prayer.

Thank you, Les and Leslie, for your unbelievable support. I am grateful. I stand in awe.

Thank you to the Happy Wives Club community that has

spread this message throughout the world that love and marriage can, should, and do go hand in hand.

Thank you Bill, Bryan, Chad, Brian, Kristen, DJ, Emily, Katy, Janene, and the rest of the Thomas Nelson crew. So honored to be on your roster.

Thank you, Jen, for gutting the first draft of this book and making it so much better.

Thank you, Heather and Much & House PR, for being a supporter of the HWC movement and this book.

Thank you to my father, who is undoubtedly smiling from above, rooting me on and making sure I never forget that people—not money and power—are the greatest commodity on earth.

NOTES

DAY ONE: THE PLAN FOR A HARMONIOUS MARRIAGE
1. Research by Dr. Helen Fisher using data from the Statistical Office of the United Nations. See Helen Fisher, "The 7-Year Itch? Make It Four!" *Happen*, Match.com, accessed September 9, 2014, http://www.match.com/magazine/article/9054/.
2. Ibid.

DAY TWO: WHAT MOST ARGUMENTS ARE REALLY ABOUT
1. Max Lucado, *It's Not About Me* (Nashville: Thomas Nelson, 2004), 7.

DAY THREE: THROW OUT YOUR PLAN B
1. *Time* magazine was the original source, but the article is no longer online, just quotes on other sites (e.g., http://www.lifeleadership .com/8Fs/Arcticles/tabid/67/EntryID/397/CatID/4/en-US/login).

DAY FIVE: PAY ATTENTION TO THE ORIGINAL EMOTION
1. *The Oprah Winfrey Show*, January 25, 2010, © Harpo Inc.

DAY EIGHT: DREAM A NEW DREAM
1. Maggie Reyes, "The Definition of a Happy Marriage," March 12, 2014, http://www.happywivesclub.com/the-definition-of-a-happy -marriage/.

NOTES

DAY TWELVE: EMBRACE A DAY OF REST
1. Ben Tinker, "The Importance of a 'Stop Day,'" CNN.com, January 11, 2013, http://www.cnn.com/2013/01/11/health/sleeth-take-day-off/.
2. *Time* magazine, June 6, 1983, cover story.
3. Andrew Weil, "Dealing with Stress," http://www.drweil.com /drw/u/ART00694/Stress.html.

DAY FOURTEEN: RELEASE YOUR EXPECTATIONS OF PERFECTION
1. Gary D. Chapman, "The 5 Sides of Intimacy," *Today's Christian Woman*, September 2008, http://www.todayschristianwoman.com /articles/2008/september/13.24.html.

DAY SIXTEEN: GET A CLUE (THEN A CUE)
1. "Divorced 'Real Housewives': More Than Half of All Current Cast Members Are Divorced," HuffingtonPost.com, April 1, 2013, http:// www.huffingtonpost.com/2013/04/01/divorced-real-housewives-_n _2993724.html.

DAY SEVENTEEN: FIVE WORDS OF PREVENTION
1. "Iyanla Vanzant's 3 Personal Prayers," Oprah.com, http://www.oprah .com/own-super-soul-sunday/Iyanla-Vanzants-3-Personal-Prayers-Video.
2. "Thomas Edison and Menlo Park," The Thomas Edison Center at Menlo Park, accessed December 24, 2013; "Anthony, Susan B," *The Social Welfare History Project*, accessed December 24, 2013; "10 Homeschooled Celebrities," CNN, April 23, 2009, accessed December 24, 2013, http://www.florence-nightingale.co.uk/cms/index.php /component/content/article/77-florence-nightingale/florence -introduction/4-florence-introduction; Sharon A. Takiguchi, May 7, 2012, "Historical Woman: Florence Nightingale—The Lady With the Lamp," *Yahoo! Voices*, accessed December 24, 2013, "Biography of Franklin D. Roosevelt," Franklin D. Roosevelt Presidential Library and Museum, accessed December 24, 2013; "American President: Woodrow Wilson: Life Before the Presidency," Miller Center of Public Affairs, retrieved December 24, 2013.

DAY EIGHTEEN: KEEP A SCORELESS MARRIAGE
1. Alisa Bowman, "How Not to Keep Score,"

ProjectHappilyEverAfter.com, January 11, 2012, http://www
.projecthappilyeverafter.com/2012/01/how-not-to-keep-score/.

DAY TWENTY: HONOR YOUR FAMILY
1. *Monster-in-Law*, screenplay by Anya Kockoff, 2005 movie distributed by New Line Cinema.
2. "High Divorce Rate in India? Blame Mom-in-laws," *OneIndia.com*, May 27, 2009, www.oneindia.com/2009/05/27/itsofficial-moms-in-law-are-chief-cause-of-divorce.html.
3. Jumana Farouky, "Mother-in-Law Problems: They're Worse for Women," *Time*, December 4, 2008, http://content.time.com/time/world/article/0,8599,1863282,00.html.

DAY TWENTY-TWO: THE NUMBER ONE REASON FOR STRIFE
1. *Money*, June 2014, 66.
2. Zig Ziglar, http://www.goodreads.com/quotes/2636-many-marriages-would-be-better-if-the-husband-and-wife.
3. Cybele Weisser, "Richer Together," *Money*, June 2014.

DAY TWENTY-FOUR: FOLLOW THE 10/90 RULE
1. Robert Kiyosaki, *Rich Dad Poor Dad* (Scottsdale, AZ: Plata Publishing, 2011), 81.
2. Ibid.
3. *Fortune*, April 1, 2002, 64.

DAY TWENTY-FIVE: MORE MONEY, LESS STUFF
1. "Level the Financial Playing Field," *Money*, June 2014, 70.

DAY TWENTY-SIX: REDEFINE THE AMERICAN DREAM
1. James Truslow Adams, *The Epic of America* (Boston: Little Brown & Co., 1931), 214–15.
2. Adams, *The Epic of America*, 2nd ed. (Greenwood Press, 1931), 405.
3. "Over 50 Percent of Americans Struggle with Home Affordability," http://www.marketwatch.com/story/over-50-of-americans-struggle-with-home-affordability-2014–06–03.
4. John Morgan, "Hart Research: Home Ownership Fades as

American Dream," June 4, 2014, *MoneyNews*, Read Latest
Breaking News from Newsmax.com, http://www.Moneynews.com
/Personal-Finance/Hart-Research-Home-Ownership-American
-Dream-Mortgage/2014/06/04/id/575253/#ixzz3LdEKUEWT.
5. 2014 How Housing Matters Survey, conducted by Hart Research
Associates, http://www.macfound.org/press/press-releases/housing
-challenges-real-many-americans-finds-2014-how-housing-matters
-survey.

About the Author

Fawn Weaver is a *New York Times* and *USA Today* best-selling author, a businesswoman, a marriage advocate, and the founder of the Happy Wives Club, a community of close to one million women in 110 countries. HappyWivesClub.com is an upbeat blog dedicated to positively changing the tone about marriage. It has attracted more than ten million visitors and was twice named the number one marriage website by the readers of About.com.

Fawn and Keith, her husband of eleven years, live in Agoura Hills, California.